I Made the Sunflower

Living Each Day Boldly and Beautifully Centered

Deborah Dutton

TRILOGY
PROFESSIONAL PUBLISHING MEETS POWERFUL PROMOTION

A wholly owned subsidiary of **TBN**

DEDICATION

I dedicate this book to my three sunflowers:
Terah, Taneia, and Tessa.

Stay bold, brave, and beautiful!

ENDORSEMENTS

Deborah Dutton is not only one of our most esteemed Christian writers but a dear friend who lives every word she writes. I can confidently say her book will change your life. Through "I Made the Sunflower," you will realize God can become the center of your life "only when you are in the center of your life with Him." Through this book, you will also learn how to "take a starring role in a world that may try to knock you off your stage," overcome the infection of perfection, and trust that "your unique gifts are all that God needs to fulfill His plan for your life." I promise "I Made the Sunflower" will make God's work through you become more memorable, just as this book will become impossible for you to forget!

—Ms. Cynthia Wickwire
Director of Women's Ministries and Heels
Conference of TurningPoint Church, Fort Worth, Texas

I walk into the stores in Texas in July, and the sunflowers are on sale for $4.99 a bunch. They are everywhere in the store's front. I buy two packets because as I walk into my home for the next few days, and hopefully a week, they will make me smile!

Then I got a call from Deb Dutton telling me about the sunflower and asking if I could write an endorsement for her book. I jumped at the chance because she enlightened me about the sunflower and its relevance to the lives of women. This analogy of the sunflower spoke volumes to me, the illustration of balancing our lives as women and giving ourselves the permission to "take center stage"!

I know women will thoroughly enjoy being challenged, encouraged, critiqued, and motivated through this book. You must own your creativity, failure, success, pain, defeat, shame, and the glory of Jesus in your life. I wish Deb Dutton every success with this new creativity of putting into expression the love and challenge to be the light in the darkness of this present age we live in.

—Dr. Marina McLean,
Founder of Mega Women Ministries

This book is a page-turner. I love Deborah Dutton's conversational writing style, which draws the reader into her stories and illustrations.

I especially admire Deb's passion for giving God the glory in all she does and for her love of the Bible. The timeless principles in "I Made the Sunflower" are for women of all ages, and the message, uniquely portrayed through a sunflower, is needed at such a time as this.

—Sharon Hill
Founder OnCall Prayer, Inc, OnCallPrayer.org
Author, Prayer Coach, Mentor, and Speaker

TABLE OF CONTENTS

FOREWORD

If you are like me and read her highly successful *I Made the Rainbow*, you have been counting the days until the release of her newest book, *I Made the Sunflower*. Our wait has been rewarded royally!

I Made the Sunflower gives us a fresh perspective on our walk with the Lord. Her choice of comparing women to glowing sunflowers is excellent. She explains how the center of these flowers is as distinctive and large as we should be when we take center stage in our lives for Christ. As you read, you will learn how to blossom and present your unique, God-made handiworks to every person you meet. When we live with confidence and purpose, our distinctive talents will glow like yellow petals of light.

This is one of the best books I've read. It demands us to "dig" deep into our souls. Deborah's "Dig in the Soil" self-help sections differ from "reflections" in other mentoring books. We are asked hard questions, but, more importantly, we are asked to generate individual answers by developing personalized action plans (based on the new principles we just learned) and putting these plans to work deliberately and immediately. What a joy it will be for you to take these unique self-tests that translate into life-altering growth. For example, do you know the five primary petals in your life? Sunflowers have many petals but rely only on their five major ones.

Deborah wrote this book especially for young women, mothers, and ministry leaders. Her goal is to help us overcome real-life issues and assist others to do so—and she delivers!

Whatever challenges you face, by the time you finish reading *I Made the Sunflower*, you will have learned to:

- Consistently, move forward facing the "Son," just as sunflowers move continuously from east to west as the sun advances across the sky.

- Become a bolder Christian so you can stand out for Christ, just as sunflowers take their stances above other flowers in an arrangement.

- Trust God's plan for your life, just as sunflowers trust bees to pollinate them so they can grow stronger.

- Never hide behind insecurities, just as sunflowers never hide behind smaller flowers;

- Celebrate your uniqueness, just as every sunflower is an original (no two are alike);

- Mature in your Christian walk so that you can plant God's abundant seeds, just as sunflowers produce seeds only when they mature;

- Constantly produce fruits of the Spirit, just as sunflowers produce more seeds than any other flower;

- Let your seeds of faith become crowning glories in your walk with God, just as sunflower seeds are crowned the top health food in the world; and

- Grow deep roots and pursue better plans constantly, like sunflower roots continuously make the soil better by enabling it to hold more moisture.

Deborah's stories show us that when our hearts are fully surrendered to the Master, and we are happy with the beautiful vessels of God's handiwork in which we have been placed, God can actualize His plans for our lives. She proves that our way to fulfillment is not plodding down the road of "just working harder," demanding our own way, or manipulating others.

Personally, I needed to learn that (1) to stand stubbornly is good when I speak up for truth and righteousness; (2) to hide my talents means I am shying away from giving God His glory; (3) to check all things out and never jump to conclusions; and, (4) to leave life-altering, meaningful deposits in the hearts of others, I must sink more deeply into my Father's lovingkindness.

My prayer is that you experience spiritual growth as I did by reading *I Made the Sunflower*.

—Cathy Collins Block, PhD
Emeritus Professor of Texas Christian University
Director of Communications, Heels Conference,
TurningPoint Church
Leadership Team, Kingdom Women,
TurningPoint Church

CHAPTER ONE:

THE CENTER

Have you ever tried to whistle through giggles? I have. It was 1974, and I entered the sixth-grade talent show. I decided my friends should enter as well, and for our talent, we would do a salute to the Vietnam troops. With our plan in motion, we decided to dress in fatigues and whistle the "Colonel Bogey March," composed in 1914 by Lieutenant F. J. Ricketts.[1] We thought with excitement that this would take a great deal of talent and guts to stand in front of parents, teachers, and classmates while whistling. The cheerleaders performed their perfect routine before us, and then we took the stage. There we were, seven girls frozen on stage and unable to get a single tweet out. But we had a sound all right—the sound of giggles.

Red-faced, the music teacher stopped the song and gave us one more shot to get our act together. As we began again, I felt the giggles coming up my throat, and I knew this was a hopeless feat. Suddenly, out of our group, one girl moved into the spotlight and stepped up to center stage as a clear sound came from her puckered lips. Quickly, we all joined in, and somehow, we made it to the finish line. I was ever grateful for her bravery that day.

Often, I reflect on this moment, and I realize that many times I've not taken center stage in my life. As women of faith, we are taught to be God-centered, but what does it look like to be a God-centered woman? Is He in the center, and we work around Him? Do we place Him in the middle of everything? Acts 17:28 (KJV) reads, "For in Him we live and move and have our being..." The only way God can be in the center of your life is when you are in the center of your life *with* Him. Being centered is when you boldly take center stage with the hope of His glory shining forth through you.

We love when our children get the lead in a play, have a dance recital, or make the big play for the team. Our Father blessed us with life and life more abundantly, so why do we cow down, play dumb to who we truly are, or try to explain away the joy and peace that we have in knowing we are the King of kings' child?

In John 20:17 (NLT), "Jesus said, 'Do not cling to me, for I have not yet ascended to the Father. Go instead to my brothers and tell them, 'I am ascending to my Father and your Father, to my God and your God.'" Jesus had just walked out of the tomb after being dead for three days, and He was talking to Mary Magdalene. Jesus told her He was going to see her Father, her God. Did she know before that garden moment she was God's daughter? She had carried such painful issues that only Jesus could deliver her from.

Jesus healed her wounded heart, delivered her of seven demons, and taught her how to love others. No amount of anxiety medications could have helped her. Only the Savior could set her free. What love she had for Him.

I love the fact that Jesus chose a woman to first reveal Himself to at the tomb. Jesus knew she would go with great excitement and tell the others. In the garden, He had to command her not to hold on to Him, and you can sense her deep emotion. She wanted to touch Him, to bury her head at His feet, and to wrap her arms around her Redeemer— her living Savior. Mary's life had been forever changed and set free! He was in the center of her heart, and she had been given a life of *more*. I am like Mary Magdalene. My Savior has healed me, delivered me, and taught me how to love, yet I struggle with what it means to be *centered* with Him and what it means to shine brightly for Him. Can you relate?

YOU WANT TO BE A SUNFLOWER

I remember it like it was yesterday. I was standing in my living room, struggling to enjoy the attention that the success of my first book was bringing me, when, suddenly, God dropped in my heart the image of a sunflower. As I quieted my heart to listen, I realized God was inviting me to understand a new aspect of Himself as the light of our lives and a new aspect of how He made me as His daughter. God wanted me to shine like a sunflower that confidently took center stage and unapologetically reflected His light. At that moment, I knew that not only was God asking me to shine, but He was asking me to lead His daughters on a journey of shining and standing tall in His light as His precious sunflowers. God made sunflowers to reflect the sun bravely and shine boldly. And that is how He made you and me. We are called to shine brightly.

Sunflowers are beautiful and cheerful, with full bright petals. It's almost impossible not to be mesmerized by a field of them as they sway in waves of bright yellows and golds. Each sunflower shoots straight up towards the sun— bold, confident, and unwavering. A sunflower receives life and gives life, and in youth, it always faces the sun. Young sunflowers face the east in the morning and then face the west in the evening. The sunflower placed in any arrangement shows up and shows off. There is no hiding its beauty. It overshadows all the other flowers with its large center and bright golden petals. It takes center stage in any display, and the other flowers must complement its glory, playing only a supporting role.

PERMISSION TO SHINE

I've been a part of many design projects over the years. One design project was a master suite with a budget of 150,000 dollars. I designed it with a custom onyx bathtub, two water closets (toilet in the closet), a circular glass shower, two fireplaces, a sitting room, and three closets with a dressing room. We even designed a desk in the bath area, so the client could plan her day in the mornings while having her hair and makeup done. This client spared no expense. However, I have also worked on a master suite that was a twelve by twelve space with a small closet and bath. This client's budget was 20,000 dollars. Both clients had the same talented interior designer (me), and both jobs were of equal hourly value in price. I gave the same care and paid the same attention to detail for each project. I desired for the space to be all it could be, no matter the client or cost. While the smaller space had constraints on size and funding (this defined the outline of where I could go with the design), in the end, I loved working with and facing the challenges of a small-budget project. I enjoyed the freedom of the larger space as well.

I valued each space the same. They were equal in my heart's desire to make the best space possible for each client, regardless of the price. Your heavenly Father values His daughters all the same. Your size, finances, education, and ethnic background have nothing to do with your value to the King or His desire to make you shine. You are a masterpiece, and He is molding and shaping you daily. Your job is to understand your value and to understand that you are the star of the show. Be bold, be brave, and be *centered*. I'm not saying to be selfish or prideful, but I feel as women, we need to become the bright stars our divine Designer wants us to be. Stars get their light from the sun, and they are the reflection of that great light. When we walk in the "Son's" beam, we shine bold and bright! Own it, girl!

THE LIGHT

"When Jesus spoke again to the people, he said, 'I am the light of the world. Whoever follows me will never walk in darkness but will have the light of life'" (John 8:12, NIV). Are you dimming your light? There are animals in nature that need light to survive. For example, the moonlight draws the puffins to their nesting ground, and the sea turtles need reflecting light to show them the way into the sea, where they can grow and mature. However, sometimes the city lights confuse these small babies, and they end up going the wrong way. The animals need light, but they need help to follow the *right* light. Environmentalists help these small baby animals survive by turning off lights at night so they can follow the true light.

Similarly, we need to turn off the wrong lights so that we can shine with truth. No wonder social media draws us in—that light that plays a large part in our everyday lives. I remember a time when maybe I would look through a magazine once a week, or while visiting a friend, I would look through the photo album showing her family's last vacation. We are visual people, and God designed us to be that way. But our minds need a break.

Think of just today; how many images have you viewed? We carry with us an instant tool of discontentment, and in a moment, it can take our value. Twitter, Facebook, Pinterest, Instagram—we cannot resist looking at our friends and family's posts, catching small moments of their lives. We can pull up photos of perfectly designed rooms or a model dressed in the latest fashion trend with filters.

You may be having a great day and decide to check out a girlfriend's latest post from the evening before, and there's Amy with her hubby at a star restaurant, a dozen red roses on the table and around her neck, a new diamond necklace! The caption, "Wonderful evening with my man. Dave surprised me with a dinner date. I'm so in love!"

You are thinking of last night with *your* man; he passed out in the recliner from working long hours. He has never surprised you with a dinner date, and he barely selects a birthday card, but he's a great guy, works hard, knows how to manage the family's budget, loves you with all his heart, and serves in the local church.

You may not know it, but Amy's family is having money issues, and her marriage is struggling. You feel a deep discontentment moving into your heart, pulling you from the light of *truth*. When your man comes home feeling blessed because he had a good day at work, you are short with him. Then he feels like he did something wrong. He does not know that your light has been dimmed and the joy of his love has been robbed from your heart. Now, your husband feels shame and failure. Vain imaginations turn the *true* light off every time. Like the sea turtle, you may need to turn off the wrong lights so that you can follow the true light—Jesus—and safely find your way home.

THE GREAT DESIGN

"The Lord is my light and my salvation; whom shall I fear? The Lord is the stronghold of my life; of whom shall I be afraid?" (Psalm 27:1, ESV). I watched an interview with a well-known artist, and when asked how he knew when his works were complete, he answered, "They never are. I just let them go." When I think about the Father and how He is molding and making our lives shine for His glory, I see how *our* masterpiece is never complete. God is always adding things to our lives and working to bring out their beauty. Then He lets us shine! He lets us go, and we reflect His handy work. Do we accept the vessel He placed us in? Are we happy to be in His care? Are our hearts fully surrendered to the Master, knowing His design plan is perfect, even if the canvas seems marked or flawed?

Recently, I purchased a well-known designer handbag. I felt stylish, and I wanted to look successful. I thought interior designers should reflect taste and style, and the bag would add a statement—"hire me!" I placed my stuff inside my new purchase and headed out to the local town center. I had not walked far when I passed a well-dressed lady carrying my new handbag! So, I darted into a boutique. As I walked in, something caught my eye. To my surprise, coming straight toward me was, again, my handbag in all its detail. Quickly, I walked across the shop and then out the door. I had lost all desire for shopping, so I headed for the parking lot. But, as I looked up, while the details were different, someone was passing me with a handbag by the same designer, and it shared the same fabric and print.

I went home, took my stuff out, went straight to the store, and returned my designer bag. It was no longer of value to me. Why had it lost its value? Wasn't it still the same high price and the same well-made design? Nothing about the bag had changed, but there is nothing more boring than sameness. As a designer, the excitement of creating something new makes my day. I still love a well-designed handbag, do not misunderstand. But your value comes from the love the Father has for you and the unique way He designed you. The Master loves to make you all you can be—not the same.

TRUST ISSUES

Sometimes, we may find it hard to trust the plan that God has for our lives, and discontentment can sneak its way into our hearts, dulling our shine and distracting us from God's light. Discontentment is a symptom of a heart that has lost sight of the true light. A disease can be in someone's body, but they might be unaware until symptoms show up. To find the cure, they must find the root cause. Discontentment is a lot like a disease. We need to look for the root cause to remove it.

I know the pains of discontentment. All for my desire to have a better life, I worked harder, demanded my way, and manipulated others. But deep in my dissatisfied heart, I discovered the root was simply a lack of trust. I did not understand that the simple act of trusting God's goodness, His plan, would cure my woes. "Woe is me; I'm not enough! I'm lacking this skill, not got that talent... I'm just—*not equipped for that calling.*" As you move into a place of trusting God, the dull ache of discontentment will leave, and the contented, trusting heart will assure you that you have all you need for today. Stay in your center with the Father.

GIVE A LITTLE WHISTLE

In the Disney movie *Pinocchio*, the song "Give a Little Whistle" has always been a favorite of mine. In the same way, when you are tempted to be dissatisfied or ungrateful, turn your eyes to Jesus.

Hebrews 12:2 (NLT) reads, "We do this by keeping our eyes on Jesus, the champion who initiates and perfects our faith. Because of the joy awaiting him, he endured the cross, disregarding its shame. Now he is seated in the place of honor beside God's throne." So, maybe you don't need to whistle, but I think the idea might be to *give a little prayer!* When you are feeling knocked off your center, focus your eyes back on the Father. When we put our focus on the master Designer, not only do we reflect His light, but His light also changes us. We will be changed into the image of what we are observing. So we may need to ask, *Am I observing God's Word? Am I observing His presence?* As we keep our eyes on Jesus, our trust in Him will increase. "The LORD is my strength and my shield; my heart trusts in him, and he helps me. My heart leaps for joy, and with my song I praise him" (Psalm 28:7, NIV). When we trust God, we shine His light, and we remain *centered.*

ADDING VALUE

As a young girl, I desired to have my ears pierced. I knew I would never get my parents' permission, so I enlisted the help of a friend. I mean, how hard could it be to put a hole in your ear? So, my friend got ice cubes and a potato, and we decided a large safety pin would do the job. The only issue is that the pin went in at an angle. When I placed my earrings through the holes, they went in at an angle. They also became infected.

Having an infection was not good, and I knew I had to tell my mom. So, I went to her office at our family business, where my friend's mom was the secretary. Walking into their shared office, I devised a plan. My issue was trying to find the best way to tell my mom I had done something she disapproved of—yet again. So, I began, "Mom, did you ever do something that your mom didn't approve of?" Talk about imagination! All kinds of things went through her head.

She replied, "Deborah Bernice, just what have you done? Tell me what!"

"I've pierced my ears," I finally blurted.

"Is that all?" Mom said with great relief. But my dad— the look he gave me was a different story.

"Why did you do that?" He wanted to know.

I am a trained life coach, and during my training, they taught me never to ask a client "why." *Why did you do that?* This question simply stops the flow of conversation, and there is judgment in the word "why." In coaching, answers should come from the client. Even if, as a coach, you see things clearly, you should never give them the answer. You may see it so clearly, but growth is all about self-discovery. Change comes from the desire for it and seeing the issue for yourself. The goal is to help them come up with the game plan on their own while you encourage them along the way. Today, I'm going to break some rules. But before I do, I want you to know that during each chapter, I'm going to ask you to "dig in the soil."

The imagery here is that of gardening. You are destined to be a sunflower that is center stage and shining. And the sunflower will help us better understand ourselves and our needs. In the same way that sunflowers need healthy soil to grow, you and I need healthy soil. One way a gardener helps the soil to be healthy is by working the dirt and aerating it. Mixing the soil and taking out old growth is the same for you and me. We can "dig in the soil" by asking ourselves hard questions and then reflecting on our answers.

DIG IN THE SOIL

Let's ask some *why* questions, "Why do we compare ourselves with our friends? Why do we feel discontented by someone's post? Why do we overspend using a week's paycheck to buy a designer handbag? Why do we have wrong relationships, addictions, and self-doubts? Why are we taking five selfies a day, feeling we need to post all our thoughts and ideas? Why are we getting upset at the little things—feeling less than others?" Take whatever issue you are facing (select just one) and ask yourself the *why* question—"Why did I do that?"

Once, there was a TV show that had a little guy named Steve Urkel, and he would often say, "Did I do that?" Now, I'm going to give you my answer. I'm going to tell you why

I pierced my ears and now have holes in them that are at an angle. This is the answer to why we do a lot of things that go outside the boundaries of our lives or even go outside of the Father's will for us. The answer is *value.* We desire and have a need for value. God created us for value, and we add it as best we can, even if by false means. Our heavenly Father wants to give us true riches and true value.

Eve, what perfect value she had. As a woman, she daily walked and talked with the divine Creator, God. But one day, something happened, and she was no longer content with whom she was. The Bible tells us her eyes were opened. I believe she and Adam saw their humanity. And ever since, we have fought to see our spirituality. Look closely; Eve was the same. God had seen her every day as she was. But now she hid from Him—she lacked value. You will never be more valuable to God than you are at this second. There is nothing you can do to make yourself more valuable to Him. He paid the price for you. It has not changed, and the price is still the same. Are you hiding—afraid—not shining in the "Son's" light because of feeling a lack of value? Are you not allowing His light to shine on your life, feeling naked? I hope you understand this journey we are on. A journey we all share equally in importance and equally not—our humanity is our shared humility. Our spirituality is our shining birthright and gift. Fully receive God's value of love and light.

Shine and shine brightly! Be the star that you already are. Boldly take center stage in your life. Receive your true value and hold that head high. Let the Father's value show forth. Embrace the scars, and don't fear the flaws. Let the world know how you bravely live each day with bold faith. Take your starring role and see the light flow from your heart. Then you will feel centered, and you will know how to live centered in a world that wants to knock you off your stage. None of us looks good in fig leaves.

Many things in life can knock us out of our center: an orphan spirit, lack of trust, hurts, unforgiveness, bitterness, wounds, and memories. Keep in mind who you surely are. Let the shine flow through your heart. Allow God to center you in Him and on the path He has set before you.

Center yourself so you can find the value in each day. Honor the Master through all the gifts and talents He has given you and all the value you have. Knowing the why won't matter anymore. Now, you can say, "Why not? Why not me? I can live blessed and not broken. I can be highly favored and love unconditionally. I can be bold with my children and declare the truth. I can trust in the light that God has given me, no matter how bright and bold He is asking me to be. To love being me is to love the Master's plan and to walk in it with victory." Bravely shine, girls! Shine, shine! Life challenges may have tried to knock you out of your center. You may have heard the saying, "That knocked me for a loop!" But you can loop around and come back more centered than ever before.

SURRENDER TO VICTORY

I'm amazed at the story of a young woman named Elizabeth Smart. At fourteen, she was taken from her family home and exposed to deplorable and abusive living conditions and scary emotional pain. She walked through a nightmare that would have turned many others into forever victims. Thankfully, Elizabeth was found nine months later and returned home.

Her mother, with wise words, helped her find her center, but it didn't happen overnight. In part, her mom told her that her captors didn't deserve another second of her life, "So be happy and move forward." Her mom didn't want Elizabeth to give any more of herself to those evil people. They had taken enough. I feel the reason Elizabeth's mom could be such a great help and support to Elizabeth was that she had stayed centered throughout the kidnapping, with the media frenzy surrounding the family. She had stayed true to her center, true to her faith. I could understand staying in bed, losing hope. But Elizabeth's mother knew she had children to care for and a home to run. I know the thought of her daughter never left her mind or heart. She had to trust and move forward herself. Did she pray and have bad days? Yes, but she never lost faith or hope for her daughter's return. Also, Elizabeth could have allowed that season to become her center, but she rose above it. Today, she shines, and her life is committed to protecting children. She uses her experience as a platform to help others not become victims but victors.

No, despite all these things, overwhelming victory is ours through Christ, who loved us. And I am convinced that nothing can ever separate us from God's love. Neither death nor life, neither angels nor demons, neither our fears for today nor our worries about tomorrow—not even the powers of hell can separate us from God's love. No power in the sky above or in the earth below—indeed, nothing in all creation will ever be able to separate us from the love of God that is revealed in Christ Jesus, our Lord.

Romans 8:37–39 (NLT)

God is our center. We are not separate; we are one. What is keeping you from your center or from the plan you know He has for you? Don't let the enemy knock you out. Past pains may have knocked you for a loop, so to speak, maybe for a large part of your life, but you can overcome the pain, and you no longer need to allow it to have a front-row seat. Hasn't it taken enough?

Elizabeth's mother's words set her on a path of healing. I'm not saying it was easy. How do we overcome loss and hurt? How do we stay front and center when life may punch us down? We know a Savior who is with us, and He brings us wholeness. Through Him, we find healing. He tells us, "Don't give any more of yourself to shame and pain—not one more second, My sweet daughter." We can have victory because He was victorious. He was right in the center of that cross, knocked down but not out. What a victorious comeback—front and center. And now, we can find victory and wholeness because He did!

CHAPTER TWO:

PETALS

I loved to play dress-up as a child. Mom would pick up used formal dresses, hats, and bags from the Goodwill store. I made my brothers play dress-up too. I know I should stop right now and write an apology to them both for scarring their childhood. But they made adorable little ladies and did not seem to mind their big sister's attention. I would use Mom's hairpieces, she called them rats, made by adding her own hair inside hair nets. She added them to her hair for Pentecostal updos. I had adorable twin little brothers, James and Wayne. I can thank goodness Mom didn't wear makeup! When we played, I was always the star, wore the best dress, and had the prettiest baby doll. I had no trouble being the center of attention then. Then life happened, and the brave little girl who deserved the best allowed her star to fade—troubles came, and I grew fearful.

Second Corinthians 4:17 (NLT) says, "For our present troubles are small and won't last long. Yet they produce for us a glory that vastly outweighs them and will last forever!" The small stuff we hide under, the little stresses. Things like, "I can't be effective in this ministry"; "I could never shine in that church; it's so large, it's too hard." "I'm not gifted in speaking." "How can I ever become a singer, songwriter, etc.?" I'm a failure as a mom and a wife." "I don't know how."

Do you know how many times I hear "I don't know how"? I wish women would just say, "I'm scared to do that." "I'm afraid to talk to my teen about that." "I'm afraid if I fully loved my husband in that way, I would get hurt." "I could never ask my boss to lighten my load, even though I'm working overtime and baking cupcakes for every office birthday and event." These are all statements that I hear. Thankfully, I can share that one lady went to her boss, bravely explained her overworked conditions, and received an assistant.

What does being the glory star of your life look like? How uncomfortable are you with the word "self-centered" living in this spotlight called your life? What does it look like to be the bright star Christ made you to be? When you wake up in the morning, you are to put on sunglasses and a dressing gown and walk into your kitchen, where coffee awaits you. Your husband will tell the maid you're up and that the children said, "Please tell Mommy we love her," as they left for school perfectly dressed and on time. Ha, we all wish! I'm not talking about being your own celebrity but about being His.

When we get in the center of our lives, and His essence is with us, life becomes balanced. If you place anything other than you and Him in the center, it just will not work. You will become lost and overwhelmed, and the path each day will be unclear. Your relationships, career, hobbies, talents, stuff, home, etc., all the things of life must come outward like petals from the center. You get to decide how many petals you have. There are seasons when our petals change or increase: a new baby, a job that is challenging, getting married, illness, or moving. But your petals should never become your identity. We should not hide behind the petals in our lives. All things should play a supporting role in whom God made us to be.

DIGGING IN THE SOIL

Many are uncomfortable with living in the spotlight of life, being the star of their show. Let's find our level of discomfort. Say one through ten. One: you are good to go; you feel no less than good enough. You know who you are and feel self-assured, as well as great peace and wholeness in your spirit! Five: you have unsure emotions; "I just do not know" rings in your mind. Discontentment sets in daily, and guilt speaks to your heart more than peace. A ten: you are so full of fear and doubt. No peace: life is so out of control, not knowing where to begin. You feel lost living a 911 lifestyle just trying to stay afloat. Can I tell you our number does not matter? The heavenly Father cares not if you are five, seven, or nine. His heart's desire is that we all become number one, and in His eyes, we are.

LITTLE STAR

I have a sweet friend who, when she was small, was another Shirley Temple. Talented and so adorable, she could dance and sing and won many beauty pageants at a young age. As she grew up, dance lessons, singing lessons, and pageants became her mom's obsession. She was the center of her life. Trophies and crowns lined the living, dining room, and her tiny bedroom walls. There were pageant photos and sashes hanging everywhere. When we visited my friend's home, her mom showed off the latest costumes and pageant dresses and played for us the latest videos. Her mom did not buy new clothes for herself, and their home was neglected. They pushed her sweet brother into the background while long-term goals were set for her to become Miss USA. Every year was planned out for her to win the title. She had a winning walk, and hopes were high, but this was not to be.

I'm not saying, "Don't give your child dance lessons or allow them to enjoy a beauty contest." But these are the small petals of life. All the people and things that make life lovely grow out of the center of your life, but they should not become your center. When we understand that we reflect our Father, then we walk a new way. As a star, I know I reflect the Most High, and I care about that reflection in the most excellent way.

When you go out the door with an "I couldn't care less attitude," you may start to feel out of place, and your behavior will change as you lose sight of all God has for you. But what would a shining star do? You may no longer want to "just get by" in your home environment, and you may discover great rewards in everyday order. As we allow ourselves to let His light shine through, we gain grace for self-care and each other. You may have a strong standard that you feel reflects the Father, but others may not. Still, His grace can flow through you. It is a great gift to walk in freedom from judgment. "Judge not, that you be not judged. For with what judgment you judge, you will be judged: and with the measure you use, it will be measured back to you" (Matthew 7:1–2, NKJV).

PETALS OF FREEDOM

When you identify your petals and you keep them in proper order, then you will experience freedom from worry and the fear of what others think of you. As a result, you will be better able to love and care for yourself. You will see the world brighter, and others will be drawn to you. I love the story of Esther, and someday we will know the rest of her journey. I think about what event orphaned her. Did she watch as her mom and dad were murdered, or did she hold her parents' hands as they passed away slowly from an illness?

The king selected her to become queen, and immediately, she stepped into her role. She shined, and she took the spotlight with grace. She may have run into a girlfriend, but I don't think she said, "I don't know why he chose me. Maybe my smile—gosh, who knows?" No, she put her shoulders back, dressed in her best robes, took baths in goat's milk, and ate a healthy diet. Then, when the time for her to shine came, she boldly went before the king and made her request known. The king granted her request because she knew who she was. Now you have been selected, and you can go boldly before the King of kings and make your request known with power and grace. Hebrews 4:16 (NKJV) reads, "Let us, therefore, go boldly to the throne of grace, that we may obtain mercy and find grace to help in time of need."

WHAT DO YOUR PETALS LOOK LIKE?

Think of all you do in a day, a week, a month. Viewing your busy life from the center out will bring a new balance. If you work outside or in the home, hire a cleaning service, even if it's one day a month. Many moms who stay home with their children need a break, so hire a babysitter, find a daycare, or trade days with a friend (one day a week, you watch all the kids, and one day a week, your friend watches all the kids). Even a nanny service now and again will add order to your home.

I mentor young women, and when I talk about viewing their lives from the center and getting outside help, I often hear, "I cannot afford it, just no way with our budget." However, I am amazed to learn that hubby has season tickets to his favorite sports team or is golfing each weekend. I recently had a talk with someone about the condition of her home and the neglect of furnishings; however, her husband was on an expensive trip to China with their daughter at the same time. I am also shocked at how children are not trained to make their beds, clean their rooms, or do laundry.

Young moms are so overworked, yet their ten-year-old cannot set the table, make French toast, or cook a simple dinner. Look at that calendar if you have no lunch dates booked with a friend or no personal care dates for yourself. Have you scheduled time for yourself? Is something besides "you" at the center of your life? And if you have no quiet time on your daily calendar, you need to make a request to King Jesus! Ask for a refresher course on your identity and a new vision of His plan and purpose for you.

POOR PETALS

I needed a ride to the hospital recently for a planned surgery and asked a sweet friend if she had the time to take me. She was so happy and excited to do so. She explained the baby would be at the sitter's, and it would be fine. As the time came, the clock passed the marked hour for pickup. I received a frantic call, "I am so sorry, I got lost taking the cat to the vet, but I am on my way, so sorry." No worries. I had planned to have plenty of time, and she only ran thirty minutes late—not a big deal. As I entered the car, I was hit by the smell of a cat. Her lap was covered in cat hair, and her baby was crying in the back seat. My friend explained, "He is hungry," as she handed a tube of baby food to the wailing child. She told me that because of the cat, she hadn't taken the time to get the baby to daycare. As we arrived, she declared, "Let me give him a bottle and change a diaper. I'm just so sorry."

Getting her sweet baby boy, covered in baby food, out of the car seat, she said again, "Oh, I am sorry. I want to come to sit with you. Give me a minute!" My heart hurt for her that day. I could see there was no joy, and what could have been an enjoyable time with a friend ended up being a scene of rush and hurry. Looking back, I wish my friend had understood the season of life she was in. Having a baby or toddler at home can feel overwhelming, but it doesn't stay that way. It's a season.

I wish my friend had understood her season and told me when I asked for a ride and for her time that she couldn't help. I would have found another ride with someone who was in a season where driving me in a tidy car and sitting with me would be easier because they either had older children, help from grandparents, or no kids at all. Again, timing and seasons are essential for us to understand. If you have a full plate, then ask God what needs to come off that plate. My friend should have taken me off her plate and said no. Saying no to me would say yes to her child, her family, and herself.

OUR FIVE PETALS

There are only five main petals on a sunflower. Yes, it looks like many more, but those petal-looking things are small extensions of the florets in the center. We must select and prune our lives, and we must let our heavenly Father prune us as well. John 15:2 (NIV) states, "He cuts off every branch in me that bears no fruit, while every branch that does bear fruit, He prunes so that it will be even more fruitful." Pruning is not a hack job. It is a delicate cutting away—a little here, a little there, the fruitless area here, and the non-life-giving activity there. Think about the draining relationship there and the endless time wasters here. Snip, snip! "For it is: Do this, do that, a rule for this, a rule for that; a little here, a little there" (Isaiah 28:10, NIV).

SMALL CHANGES

In life coaching, the goal is to first find the top issue and then set a plan for change. But the true win comes when your client breaks it down into the smallest task. Their success comes from a little change here, a little change there. Take housekeeping as an example. It's all about management. If small systems are in place and rules, the upkeep can be simple. Like making beds in the morning and having a pickup time for the entire household, little improvements over time will have a big impact. Weekly, plan a time to clear a drawer or a closet. Breaking large issues into small solutions over time will bring success.

In his book *Atomic Habits*, James Clear states:

> *Achieving a goal only changes your life for the moment. That's the counterintuitive thing about improvement. We think we need to change our results, but the results are not the problem. What we really need to change are the systems that cause those results. When you solve problems at the results level, you only solve them temporarily. To improve for good, you need to solve problems at the systems level.*[2]

The five petals of the sunflower represent grace. Let's grace ourselves with only five main areas in our lives at a time. I have pushed to have six before, and I felt overwhelmed. The word "overwhelmed" means to feel buried or drowned beneath a huge mass, to give too much of a thing to someone, or simply put—*too much*. So how do we grace our lives with balance when it's just too much? First, address five areas only and clearly define what they are.

Taking care of yourself should be a given, but if you are on a wellness plan, working out two hours a day and making special foods, then this will become a petal. Family and friends are a petal. We must plan to have a quality, fun time, making true heart connections with those we love. Maybe a hobby, writing a book, or attending classes are your petals? Caring for our homes, works, and careers are petals. Homeschooling would be its own petal. Seeing and limiting the main areas of your life to just five is essential for peace.

A great way to stay balanced is to select what petal you want to operate in and realize you may not flow in all five petals each day. Caring for an aging parent would need to be a petal. I use a letter system on my calendar to represent each of these five areas. Example: the letter "B" is for writing this book. It would be a joy for me to write every day, but I would feel out of sorts. What about my husband, grandkids, home, and design work? I must plan time to write. The book could, if I allowed it, pull at me and be on my mind all the time. I don't want to be at dinner thinking, *I wish I was writing right now.*

"F" is for the family. I love family days where the only petal all day is family. Christmas and Thanksgiving would be an example of this, where the only focus is family. Most days, I can only operate on two to three petals. Life is not about a balancing act where you try to spend the same time in every area. It's about being present in each area and fully in the moment. I wish it didn't take care and planning, but in fact, a calendar should be your best friend. You can make up a system to help you view clearly the five areas in your own life.

THE FAMILY PETALS

F: Focus on undivided attention

A: Always a priority

M: Make time for togetherness

I: It's the most important people in my life

L: Love them unconditionally

Y: You, as a family member, matter most

It's easy to have grace for others, but sometimes having grace for oneself seems selfish. See your life perfumed by grace, and do not be a petal pusher! Like the sunflower, it looks like it has a lot more petals than five. As women, we look and feel like, "I can do so much more. I can say yes to this, and I can volunteer for that." If we want each petal to shine and have value, we must select with care the areas we want to flower; then, we can flow gracefully from one to another, giving that area the full energy and attention it deserves.

LET'S DIG IN THE SOIL

Take out a piece of paper and (using your best artistic skills) draw a large flower with a circle for the center and five large bubble-like petals attached to the center. Next, name each petal. For example, you may write on the top petal "Family and Home," then (moving clockwise) on the next petal you might write "Health," followed by "Career," "Hobbies," and on the final petal you might write something like "Volunteer Work." In the center circle for my sunflower, I've written "God and Me."

Based on the values of your life, assign each petal for that area of your life: husband, children, family, friends, work, home, hobby, outreach, or ministry. You may desire to teach a class, but you know in this season, you would be overwhelmed. Add to your plate only what you can gracefully handle, and your soul will be satisfied. There are seasons where no matter how hard you try, you need to overload, but understand that God will give you the grace and strength that you need. However, also give yourself permission to say "no" so that you can say "yes" fully to life. Boundaries will set you free to live a life full of abundance. My mom had a saying, "Your eyes are bigger than your stomach," when I would fill my plate and couldn't eat it all. In the same way, *don't overload!*

WHEN DO WE HAVE TOO MANY PETALS?

I work with design clients, and my job is to help them select fabrics, colors, and furnishings for their space. But I never show up at the appointment with all my fabric books. I put together a design collection of only three fabrics and a few ideas. We define their looks and stay on the clear path of design. In *I Made the Rainbow*, I shared how to define your interior style. God has a clear design path for you, a style all yours.

When we view Jesus's earthly ministry, we see it was clearly planned. He did not run a company on the side, and He didn't have a wife or children. He was called to be dedicated to the will of His Father. His ministry was only a short season but fully focused. I can't wait to see the heavenly videos of Jesus's life that the Bible didn't share. We may be shocked to find that He fell in love but had to walk away, the great friendships He left behind, or maybe a home-building business He said goodbye to. Notice He did not call His buddies to be one of the twelve. In fact, His friends may have been negative and lacked understanding of His call.

ALL THE PETALS

Today, society tells us we can have it all; this is false. There are limits on each of us, and acknowledging this does not make you a failure. When we get clarity about our truth and limitations, then we can truly live. Out of each of us flows a plan and purpose. Some are called to live simple lives, raise amazing kids, and support a husband in his field, ministry, or dream. God's plan for some is to change the world, be an influential voice for the kingdom, or start a ministry that affects others. Examples of women world changers include Amy Ford, founder of Embrace Grace; Christine Caine, founder of the A21 Campaign to rescue girls from sex trafficking; and Suzette Munson, founder of Love 41. These ladies are sunflowers who God called out. You could be called to run a company, become an artist, or write a book. But like a bank account, we have only so many times we can overspend before we go bankrupt. Please don't live a bankrupt life. No matter what the call and plan God has for you. Make deposits of rest and mindfulness daily. Be mindful of Him, and rest in His will. Isaiah 26:3 (NKJV) reads, "You [God] will keep him in perfect peace, Whose mind is stayed on You, Because he trusts in You."

I've lived in seasons of just too much, and I've had to learn how to ask for help and how to manage my life in a better way. During my bankruptcy season, my health broke down, and my nerves were damaged. I was going ninety miles an hour, and I never said *no*. I was that person you could call and say, "We need four dozen cookies for the camp-out tomorrow; think you can make them?" I was PTA vice president and room mom, working from 11 p.m. to 2 a.m. for the airlines and getting little sleep while starting a design company.

I recall when our baby girl was born on a beautiful February day; I was in labor making heart-shaped red felt bean bags for her older sister's school party. There I was, in between contractions, hand-sewing thirty bean bags. I would have loved for someone to share with me that I was enough. I wish someone had told me about the five petals of the sunflower and that God's plan for me was simple— trust and obey. I didn't know how to surrender my worth to Him or how to find my center. "Trust and obey, for there's no other way to be happy in Jesus than to trust and obey" (song written by John H. Sammis).[3]

> *If you then are not able to do the least, why are you anxious for the rest? Consider the lilies, how they grow: they neither toil nor spin, and yet I say to you, even Solomon in all his glory was not as arrayed like one of these. If then God so clothes the grass, which is in the field, and tomorrow is thrown into the oven; how much more will He clothe you, O you of little faith?*
>
> **Luke 12:26–28 (NKJV)**

Trust Him with the petals of your sunflower. He loves you more than you will ever know. Put His plan first in your life, and things will turn out well.

CHAPTER THREE:
PRUNING IS THE ONLY WAY TO GROW

As we experience "centered" living, we see clearly what needs to go. For example, hurts and pain can become front and center in our lives. I watched as a loved one moved their mother into the center of everything. The sad part of this story is that her sweet mom had been dead for two years. However, the home was her shrine, with photos blanketing the walls, and her mother's furniture had replaced her own. Her growth stopped. Her joy stopped—her life center was loss and grief. She needed to prune her heart, but she did not know how.

Children are a relationship that must be pruned often and well, especially as they get older. With grown children, you must let go a little here and a little there until they are no longer a large petal in your life. Many mothers have issues with letting children go and grow. The mother-child relationship must be pruned many times if you want to see the growth that brings forth fruit in their lives. It is difficult for parents to allow failure to teach their child, but even more challenging is success. Mothers sometimes hold their older children back by not believing they can handle accomplishment, growth, or challenge. My three adult daughters handle life with more grace than me, and I am impressed by them. I enjoy our relationships in this season. I no longer need to let go because they are fully grown. However, I have friends who are in great distress over their adult children because they cannot prune and let go.

My friend Lydia was stressed over life when I started walking alongside her. Through prayer and many talks, we discovered her life-robbing issues. Her health, home, and life management were a daily struggle. She ran a home business and had a teenage son and a small baby girl. Evenings were the hardest time of day for her. Her hubby would arrive home, her teen had homework, dinner needed to be made, and there was bath time for the baby. Many evenings, after dinner, she would watch TV until she was numb before dragging herself to bed.

The laundry would pile up, the mail would be tossed with tension, and joy would be nowhere. She would awaken to start a new day, only to repeat the despair. Lydia knew she was not in her center, nor was she living the life her heavenly Father desired for her. Setting small goals, she began pruning. She realized the two-hour gym trip could be replaced by a thirty-minute walk with her baby and the dog. Next, she valued her crock pot, and she planned meals in the morning. She also realized that bathing the baby in the morning helped her evenings flow better. Last, she let go of some friends who wanted to talk on the phone for two hours a day—she slowly pruned away—a little snip here, a little snip there. While it was with tears sometimes, she let go of the old unproductive areas of her life and enjoyed the peace that followed.

To her surprise, Lydia had energy, and she could handle her teenager with more grace. With Lydia's guidance, her son started doing laundry and yard work. His room stayed tidy, and he made his bed regularly. She added game nights once a week for her family and even invited friends once a month. Now, mornings and evenings had a flow and a routine. Her gardening skills improved, and she could prune even more by letting go of the unhelpful "stuff" in her life. Growth can only come if there is space for it. Nothing stayed in her surroundings that did not have an obvious use and value. She then started a class in her home once a month to teach other moms the value of pruning their lives and how to use those garden clippers! "My voice You shall hear in the morning, O Lord; In the morning I will direct it to You, And I will look up" (Psalm 5:3, NKJV).

How did Lydia find joy and learn how to live in her center? She found joy by starting each day seeking the Father, recalibrating, and getting His clear vision. She declared who she was and learned how to shine. I had her take a photo of herself and draw a circle around her face. Then, she drew five petals. Naming each one, she had a clear vision of how to become the star of her show. Lydia showed up in her own life! Nothing changed. She didn't have more income, no new home, and no new job, but she changed. Lydia lost ten pounds and found time to rest and read something she loved but had set aside. She still watched TV but pruned that as well, and bubble baths and facials became a weekly treat. I ran into Lydia and her family six months later; her son standing tall, his shoulders back, greeted me with "hello." She explained to me that she had seen a big change in him, and even his grades had improved because she showed him how to move into his center and take the pruning shears to his own life.

LET'S DIG!

Get out the pruning shears and make a list of the many little things you need to cut away. Do you need to prune social media, unhealthy habits, or just all the clutter in your home? Start slow but keep clipping! Make room for new growth. Do you want to start a book project or rebuild a relationship? What needs to go so new seeds of value can have space and time? Things of value to you may include a health class, the painting lessons you wish to take, or that book you desire to write. Often, I hear it said, "I don't have time." More truthfully, we should say, "I haven't made time for that."

CAREER PETALS

I am so blessed to have three lovely daughters, and I love them all so much. When I think of cutting, hair comes to mind. We had many bad hair days in our family. Today,

I'm blessed to have my very own stylist, who is my middle daughter. She started her career at a young age by giving a couple of cousins new hairstyles and taking off her own bangs a time or two. When she was going to cosmetology school, I wanted to be a supportive mom, and I allowed her to practice on my hair. She had shown me a photo of a new look where the hair on one side went behind the ear and was fuller on the other. It looked trendy and cute. As she began to cut, I wasn't paying close attention. I expressed my concern, and she told me this was the cut I had agreed to, and it was called an asymmetrical hairstyle. She said, "Let's leave it at that." She was out of time, and I had a hairstyle I could in no way live with. With my design eye, I felt completely out of balance, and I walked around feeling like I would fall over. This hairstyle just wasn't for me. She had pruned too much, so to speak. I ended up with a cute but very short hairstyle.

Our good Gardener, Jesus, understood gardening. It all started in the Garden of Eden and ended in the Garden of Gethsemane. I'm sure His return will be in a garden. The tomb for Jesus's burial was in a garden. I was blessed with gardening grandparents. My papa Harvey always showed off his tomatoes and peppers. He planted a variety of both and made a pepper concoction so that when you opened the jar, tears would come.

On the Ohio farm, my grandpa Roark had a large garden. When we moved there from Texas, my mom tried to plant okra and black-eyed peas in Grandpa's garden, but every year, Grandpa would pull up the okra thinking they were weeds. And black-eyed peas—well, that was cows' feed to him. I have the best memories of going to the garden with my grandma Anna. With our aprons on, we would head out early and pick Kentucky wonders (green beans, if you're wondering). She would tie up her apron and fill it full, and we would pull weeds as we went. The ground was moist early in the morning, and the weeds were easy to pluck.

PRUNING WORDS

We must tend the garden of our lives just like a vegetable garden needs tending. Weeds need to be pulled early, and feeding must come daily. Words can be weeds or fertilization for our gardens. Words are sown so easily; if we aren't thoughtful, we can carelessly toss words over our gardens. Our children, husbands, and our own hearts are such tender plants. "For He who would love life and see good days, Let him refrain his tongue from evil, And his lips from speaking deceit" (1 Peter 3:10, NKJV).

We must watch not only words tossed at our loved ones but also words tossed at ourselves—words like, "I can't; there's no way." Words like these will keep you from growing. When we have self-talk that is not in alignment with God's plan, we use deceitful words that go straight to the heart. As a man thinks in his heart, so be it. Weeds choke out vision. Without vision, we will not see fruit. The late Zig Ziglar went around teaching the "I can course." He spread the word like feed for your garden, of positive thoughts, actions, and words. There are so many good Zig Ziglar quotes. My favorite is, "What you get by achieving your goals is not as important as what you become by achieving your goals."[4]

LET'S DIG IN THE SOIL!

If you had a recording of all the words you have spoken the last twenty-four hours, can you recall the weeds planted, the weeds (negative thoughts) you pulled up, or the life-giving feed you have spread? "A word fitly spoken is like apples of gold and settings of silver" (Proverbs 25:11, NKJV). "Pleasant words are like a honeycomb, sweetness to the soul..." (Proverbs 16:24, NKJV). You can never satisfy a sweet tooth, and you can never sow too many sweet words. A word sown in the right season can change a life. This is how my first book, *I Made the Rainbow*, was born. My friend, Jan Greenwood, spoke a word that unlocked my book. She planted a seed and pulled a weed.

THE MISSION TRIP OF A LIFETIME

One evening, when I was checking out my groceries at our local store, the lady in front of me turned and asked if I had been anywhere that summer. I was tired and surprised, but this total stranger was bubbly and excited to share the fact that her family had been to Belize three times this year and, in fact, had moved from California to be closer to their favorite place on the planet. "Did you know it's only a three-hour plane ride, and the water is so blue?" she shared. I was nodding my head like I knew all about it while thinking, *I just need to check out and go home to make dinner.* The checkout lady apparently had read something about the sea life there, and she joined in on this very one-sided conversation. I went home and researched Belize and all its beauty. I thought, *I'd love to go there one day* as I went off to bed.

That fall, we had an invitation to a church retreat, where they excitedly shared that our church would offer a mission trip to—yes, you guessed it—Belize! I thought that had to be God's will and plan for me. I signed up right away. But, as the months passed, I became the primary caretaker for two of our young grandchildren. Their mother was in school, and she depended on my help. With the trip a few months away, I realized it would not be possible for me to go, so I let go of the dream of my first mission trip. I called the church and blessed someone with the money I had paid and was content to be Grammie.

Some months later, my friend who managed the mission trips at our local church had returned from an Alaska trip (not a mission trip, but a fun cruise). I wanted to catch up and hear all about it, so I booked a lunch. Before we even sat down, she asked if I could go to Belize next Saturday. She explained that a couple's father was deathly ill, and they had to back out, and she needed another lady to go, or the discounts would be lost. I looked at her and said, "I'm 99 percent sure I'm going to Belize."

After I went home, I talked to my youngest daughter, who is a nurse and who has never had four days off in a row, but she did that next week. With the seven days of childcare fully covered, I got on a plane for my first mission trip. The excitement in my heart was overflowing. And to top it off, I would share a room with one of our beloved women's pastors.

Jan Greenwood is charming and full of faith. Immediately, I felt we were the best of friends. As our trip unfolded, it became clear that it was a conference. We visited a couple of villages and delivered food to local families, but our big event was meeting with business leaders from the area to give them support and guidance while establishing a relational connection.

We stayed in a large home of a local business owner, on a beach, with a maid and a chef taking care of our every need. They served us lobster, treated us to a boat ride, and we enjoyed the relaxing surroundings. Jan had to listen as I went on about how exciting it was to be on a mission trip— "When will we get to hold babies and serve the needy?" Finally, almost at the trip's end, Jan shared that this was not really a mission trip but a retreat. But I tried to convince her that it was a mission trip because we had hard times, like the van traveling through the river to get to the boat ride—that was *mission-like*, right? She just laughed as I tried to create hardship where there was none.

During our trip, I shared with Jan that I felt like I was supposed to write a book, but I didn't know how. Placing one hand on her hip, she said with a pointed finger, "Stop saying you don't know how and do it like you design a room." At that moment, the book downloaded into my mind and heart. I got off the plane, went home, and wrote the chapter outline. It took time, but four years later, my first book was published.

Words, how wonderful their power is. They bring life to a soul like gold. What could your words do for someone today? Pick up the phone and give out some uplifting, encouraging words, and it will add gold to your day too. But words can also get us into trouble. During the trip, I was allowed to sit on a board so the local businesspeople could ask questions. I did okay on how to add character to your company, show up on time, and pay your help, but then I told a man that an ice cream social would fix his problems with his employees. Let's just say I wasn't on the board the next day.

WHAT NOT TO PRUNE

As we prune, it may be easy to see what needs to go, but *what to keep* is a hard question. We all understand boundaries and that we should guard our hearts, but no one talks much about what to keep in our hearts—what to allow to stay. When we clear our homes of the negative, we need to replace it with a positive. I fill my home with love and hospitality. When we stop eating unhealthy food, we are more likely to add healthy food to our diets. But I found I was on guard too much. What had healed me and was a healthy boundary also kept me from reaching out to others. I realized this at a leadership event. A large group of women and I came together to learn how to act and respond to leadership roles in the church. On the first night, I felt the pin light hit my heart. I wanted to size everyone up; I wanted to wait and see where I fit in. Sadly, I wanted to judge. As leaders, we should be welcoming and pull others in, but letting your guard down may not be easy if someone has hurt you in the past.

I, who felt called to work with women, had to stop and look deep inside at the fact that I had pruned a little too much. I realized I needed to keep a part of my heart open and just allow love to flow. You can kill a plant if you over-prune it. I've killed a few plants in my day, and I have lost a few relationships that I valued. I love roses, and the secret to growing great roses is how you prune them. It's so easy to cut the dead part, but when you need to cut back and remove a beautiful rose for the sake of the whole bush, that can be difficult. It is challenging to prune areas in our lives that are not bad but good.

We had an old Victorian mansion on our Kauffman County farm. Behind the mansion was an old rose garden with neglected rose bushes and lots of weeds. These old roses had survived for about one hundred years, tangled and thorny, but they were still producing a few roses. I'm sure that garden was amazing in its day when care and pruning were ministered by a loving gardener—perhaps the woman of the house tenderly cut the roses to fill a vase for her home. The smell of this garden, even in its state, was lovely, but the fence was broken, and the stone path was worn. It saddened me when my dad had to clear it. There just was no way to save it. No amount of pruning could save those old roses. This garden may have been the reason I tried my hand at growing roses. I imagined I would raise beautiful roses in my garden and fill my home with their fragrant rewards. It was time-consuming, and I had to let this hobby go for more important things in my life. The store roses had to suffice.

TO PRUNE A ROSE

1. You will need gloves and clean, sharp tools like bypass shears. The Word of God is the sharpest tool. "For the Word of God is alive and active. Sharper than any double-edged sword" (Hebrews 4:12a, NIV). (Note that "sword" has "word" in it.)

2. Picking the right season to prune is important. The best time to prune will depend on which zone you live in. I live in Texas, which is zone 8. Pruning in February or March is ideal here.

3. Remove all leaves so you can examine the natural shape of the bush and the stems. Doing this will help to clear out any hibernating bugs and pests.

4. Start by cutting to the base of all dead brown branches (God prunes any of our branches that aren't fruit-bearing). Pruning helps the plant by sending nutrients to the alive places rather than the dead and decayed places.

5. Cut away branches that may tangle or cause friction with other branches (no need for competition, even with plants). Also, prune weaker branches, which would be any branch as thin as your pinky finger.

6. Prune so the final shape of the bush looks like an open mouth vase: upward reaching branches and an open center so light and air can get to the heart of the bush.

7. When pruning, make cuts at a forty-five-degree angle and about half an inch above buds.

8. Seal all cuts with a compound of your choice to protect the plant from disease.

MAKE SPACE FOR CHANGE

Marge was a sweet, elegant woman. When her husband passed away, he left her well cared for, and she set out to find purpose in a new season. Marge filled her life with service. Monday was Meals on Wheels; Tuesday after school reading program; Wednesday, she greeted at the local hospital; Thursday, she volunteered at the food bank; Friday, she visited the sick. Her life was blessed, and she had many friends and meaningful relationships because of this life of service.

One day, the lady overseeing the school reading program asked her to come on staff full-time. The program needed to grow, and they needed someone with great organizational skills. Their primary need to do outreach was to reach the older people in the area. They needed more readers for the children, and she would be a perfect fit for the job because she could directly communicate with the outreach's older groups. But embracing this opportunity would mean she had to let go of the other opportunities. Marge knew this was what she needed to do, and by letting go of other things, she took hold of this new thing—the job. The program more than doubled. She had a gift for recruiting seniors, and she knew how to reward their efforts. Marge pruned and didn't cut away anything negative or bad, but she had to let go of good in order to allow more light and air in her life.

No matter what season of life you are in, all of us can benefit from a little pruning. Take some time to ask God what you may need to lay aside right now, so you can make room for new things. The Bible tells us that God desires to take us from glory to glory. Let faith arise, and get excited about the bright future God has for you. Embrace the new by letting go of the old—a little snip at a time.

CHAPTER FOUR:

THE STEM

Like stems of a sunflower, we all grow at different rates and heights based on many factors. I grew up fast—I mean, I grew tall quickly, and I have stretch marks as proof. I remember being the tallest in my class many times. While I often heard the words, "Stand up straight, don't slump," I still have an issue with my posture. When I was growing up, most of my friends were short. For example, my maid of honor and best friend, Donise, was only four foot eleven. Donise's father was our church pastor, and she would sing, "I'm four foot eleven, but I'm going to heaven, and it makes me feel ten feet tall!" But compared to my family, I'm not that tall.

I married a tall Texan, six foot six inches. I loved that I could wear heels and still look up at him. His best friend, and our best man, was five feet two inches tall. We looked a little off on our wedding day. Our little ring bearer was only three. I remember little Darius almost did a backbend to look up at Terry. With Terry and I both bringing tall genes to the family, one of our daughters hit six feet before high school, and another is five-eleven.

Sunflowers are also tall and can range between six and ten feet on average; however, the tallest sunflower on record was measured at thirty feet. While sunflowers grow at different rates, the growth cycle typically happens within seventy to one hundred days. Researchers believe the young sunflowers have an internal clock similar to humans, which follows a twenty-four-hour cycle. A UC Davis professor and co-author says, in a press release from the university,

> *The researchers discovered the plants grow from different sides of the stem, elongating at different times of the day. The growth rate on the east versus west side of the stem varies. At night, it slowly turns back to the east. Growth rates on the east side of the stem were high during the day; the growth rate on the west side of the stem was highest at night.*[5]

Whether you are a sunflower or the tallest in your class, like me, we all grow at different rates, and spiritual growth is no different. Everyone's journey of spiritual growth and maturity is unique. Some people grow quickly, and others— well, let us just say, for them, some growth is better than no growth. My oldest daughter had growing pains, and the doctor recommended she work out with weights to help her bones catch up with her rapid growth.

Growing pains come in different forms. For example, the desire to have a baby is in many women's hearts. They long for that little bundle of joy. Soon, the birth pains are forgotten, and morning sickness is a thing of the past when we hold that little son or daughter in our arms. There is no thought of the growth to come: fussiness, sleepless nights, teething, potty training, the clothing they will go through, how many new pairs of shoes there will be, or the hours of homework. Your child eats and sleeps, and you watch them grow. There are growth pains for the teen years, too, such as driving lessons, the first car, and the cost of education. But as a good parent, you will see your sweet baby through each season of growth to adulthood.

You may have growing pains. Another way of saying it is that there may be pain in your growth. "Being confident of this thing, that He who has begun a good work in you will complete it until the day of Jesus Christ" (Philippians 1:6, NKJV). Paul and Timothy were encouraging the saints in Philippi by letting them know God was going to grow them up. God will grow you up too, and He will see you through till the end.

GROWING UP FAST

Erik, my grandson, would always say he was one year older than his actual age. He wanted to grow up so fast, and he did. He now looks down at me at six foot five, and I fit under his arm pit! No matter what age he told us, the facts were the facts. We can declare we are spiritually mature, but the facts are reflected in our everyday life. Our spiritual growth comes in waves through the dark times and the light times.

Have you ever noticed how fast changes happen with children and grandchildren? For example, one day, their pants are above their little ankles, and we think, *How did that happen? The pants fit yesterday.* And one day, we are eye to eye with them, and the next, they are looking down at us. We wonder, *How did they grow so fast?* God designed all of us to grow, and He wants us to grow as tall as possible, reaching for His Son.

Even the prophet Samuel in the Bible needed to grow both physically and spiritually, "And the boy Samuel continued to grow in stature and in favor with the LORD and with people" (1 Samuel 2:26, NIV). Not only did Samuel have to experience the growth process, but Jesus did as well. The Bible tells us in Luke 2:52 (NIV), "And Jesus grew in wisdom and stature, and in favor with God and man." We have no control over how fast we grow, and no matter how hard you think about it, you can't add inches to your height or change your growth rate. Growth will happen when we feed our souls, and growth comes when we stand firm in God.

STAND STRONG

The sunflower stem is the catalyst for growth because it brings nourishment from the soil to the flower. But the stem of a sunflower must be strong enough to support the seed head, which can grow to be heavy. The largest sunflower seed head had a thirty-two-inch diameter and grew in British Columbia. The heaviest sunflower head on record is from the United Kingdom and weighed in at almost twelve pounds.

The larger the flower head, the more seeds it will produce and the more support it will need. A stem must fit its calling to support growth. In the same way, you need a strong stem to support your growth and your calling. For some of us, having a strong stem might look like having a few good friends, having a spiritual life coach, or being actively involved in a small group. However, some of you may have a calling or gift that requires church staff support or maybe a community. What makes our stems strong will look different for us all because God made us unique. However, it is important you identify what makes you strong and what support in your life looks like. Once you have identified this, write it down in a journal or tell a close friend so you can have accountability as you actively engage in relationships and activities that make you strong.

I am amazed many times when women share with me that they have no friends. They are involved with their children, or they have great work relationships, but they have no strong women friendships they can depend on or have fun with. The value of true friendships increases with age, and happy seniors are the ones who are well-connected and social.

My ninety-seven-year-old grandmother had limited hearing and many health issues, but she always had great friendships. As she became bedridden, these friends would call on her daily. She loved playing cards and laughing with anyone who had the time. She had substantial support, love, and connection right up to the end of her life. "Therefore, put on the full armor of God, so that when the day of evil comes, you may be able to stand your ground, and after you have done everything, to stand." (Ephesians 6:13, NIV). Ask yourself, "Who is my stem, my support?" We stand because the Son commands it, and stand firm we must, but don't stand alone.

STANDING IN STUBBORNNESS

There is a story about a teacher who sent a little boy named Johnnie to the corner chair for a time out to think about his behavior. But little Johnnie didn't sit. The teacher insisted, "Sit down!" Little Johnnie continued standing. The teacher commanded, "If you don't sit in that chair, then you are going to the office!" Slowly, Johnnie sat in the chair of shame, but looking at his teacher, he exclaimed, "I'm sitting on the outside, but I'm still standing on the inside."

I recall the day my sweet baby girl decided to *stand*. She was two, and I was enjoying a visit with my friend Marlene. My friend Marlene could sew anything. She made all my baby girls' nursery bedding and helped me with many projects. I'm not sure what came over my sweet girl that day, but she stuck out her tongue at my friend. Embarrassed by her behavior, I asked her to say she was sorry. She stood her ground. "No!" Again, I said, "Well, you must say you're sorry, or you are going to stand in the corner." Again, she said, "No!" So in the corner, she went, and then I pleaded with her to say she was sorry. This went on for about forty-five minutes.

The whole thing ended with me worn out and Terah saying softly, "I'm sorry." I don't think I won that battle. When I read we are to become as a little child in the Word, I know it is talking about trust, but I think of how strong-willed a child can be—if we could stand in truth and righteousness in the same way my two-year-old did that day, what a difference we could make.

My grandpa Roark used to sing a song, "I shall not be, I shall not be moved; / I shall not be, I shall not be moved; / Just like a tree that is planted by the waters, / Oh, I shall not be moved. / Jesus is my Savior, I shall not be moved / In His love and favor, I shall not be moved; / Just like a tree that's planted by the waters, I shall not be moved." This song is based on Psalm 1:3 (NIV): "A person is like a tree planted by streams of water, which yields its fruit in season and whose leaf does not wither, and whatever they do prospers." In the same way, God doesn't want us to be moved. He wants us to put our hope and trust in Him and not doubt.

One night, when Jesus was on a boat with His disciples, a great storm rose, and the disciples were terrified they were going to die. You might say they didn't stand stubbornly on their faith in Jesus, and they let doubt move them. Waking Jesus up, they pleaded with Him to do something, and they even accused Him of not caring about them, "'Teacher, don't you care that we're going to drown?' When Jesus woke up, he rebuked the wind and said to the waves, 'Silence! Be still!' Suddenly the wind stopped, and there was a great calm. Then he asked them, 'Why are you afraid? Do you still have no faith?'" (Mark 4:38b–40, NLT). We won't be able to stubbornly stand in faith without a strong stem, and strengthening the stem is our responsibility. Romans 14:12 (NLT) tells us, "Yes, each of us will give a personal account to God." Scripture encourages us to examine ourselves and to examine what type of growth we are allowing the stem of our sunflowers to experience or not experience.

For growth to happen in our lives, we must actively engage our faith and put our trust in God. You are adding strength to your stem when you read your Bible regularly. When you spend time with friends who point you to Jesus, you are standing tall. When you are planted in a Bible-based church and a part of a healthy spiritual community, then your sunflower stem will grow.

The sunflowers' greatest burden is at the time of harvest—right before her rich seed ripens and right before the mild nutty-flavored seeds come forth. The weight of this harvest burden would make it hard for an underdeveloped sunflower to stand, but by the time the harvest comes, the stem is ready. Through time and process, the stem has grown strong, and it is ready to hold the weight of the next season. This is like our lives. God wants to bring us into new seasons of harvest and fruitfulness, but for this to happen, we must first let our stems grow strong.

There are seasons in our lives when we think we cannot stand. But our stem of support must be the truth—the truth of who we are and the truth of His plan. We will lose ground if we do not stand in truth. So ask yourself, "How strong is my stem?"

I enjoy watching talent shows. Sometimes, the contestant has a desire and a heart for singing, but their desire is greater than their talent to sing; their voice is not supporting the desire. The judges kindly help them face the truth. We must live in our truth and stand strong for our beliefs. Grandpa would say, "If you don't stand for something, you will fall for anything." Be strong and take courage—truth is the armor you need every day!

SHOULDERS BACK!

The British royal family has guidelines on how a royal should conduct themselves in public. They have many etiquette rules that guide them and set them apart. The ladies should not cross their legs over the knee, but they can cross at the ankle. Their chin must always be parallel with the ground or floor, and they can never lean back in their chair because they must sit straight.

Why does the royal family act this way? Simply because they are royal. They know who they represent, and what they represent is more than just themselves. They represent a line of royal kings, queens, duchesses, dukes, princes, and princesses. These rules and traditions are not a put-on they live by—it's who they are.

When you become a member of the royal family, you must become royal and be set apart. You must learn and take on the role because now you have a place of honor. It is no longer about you; instead, it is about the generations the royal family represents. "But you are a royal priesthood, a holy nation, God's special possession, that you may declare the praises of him who called you out of the darkness into his wonderful light" (1 Peter 2:9, NIV). You need to be set apart and carry yourself well by knowing who you are, by living in the center, and by standing tall through the dark times and the good times because you represent a royal family as well—the King of kings' royal family. You are God's special possession!

And there is royal etiquette for God's royal family as well; it's called the "more excellent way." God's way is not about power or money but about the heart. When the royal family expresses their royal behavior, it is for the love of the country and their royal leaders. In the same way, our love for our King and His kingdom will change our hearts, and our hearts' changes will be expressed outwardly. Proverbs 4:23 (ESV) reads, "Keep your heart with all vigilance, for from it flow the springs of life." This inner and outer reflection becomes who we are—an inner and outer expression of love through royal-kingdom living.

Unlike the royal family, there is no list telling you how to sit or stand, dress, or hold a teacup. But through Jesus, we receive a heart list, a list that desires to please God the Father, the One who knows we are priceless and special possessions. Knowing the truth of who you are will guide you, develop your trust, and attune you to the "more excellent way." This "more excellent way" will affect every area of your life, such as how you handle your money, relationships, and even the way you talk. Your dress code may even change, as well as your friendships. Your heart will ask, "What pleases the One who thinks I'm priceless today?" "And let us not grow weary while doing good, for in due season we shall reap if we do not lose heart" (Galatians 6:9, NKJV). Keep a heart for Him and stand in His love for you.

LET'S DIG IN THE SOIL

Stand up for your dream, your vision, and your faith. Ask, "What did last week look like? Did I feel supported and able to stand? Did the week leave me defeated and worn out? Were there any royal moments in my week? Did I feel priceless, or did I work through that lunch break? Did I skip coffee with a friend?" Maybe you stayed up late to do laundry and missed having a quiet time? Zig Ziglar once said, "If you learn from defeat, you haven't really lost."

As you ask yourself these questions and reflect on your answers, don't feel defeated if you have fallen short. This is your royal journey. No one can change the direction but you. Each day, view yourself as the King's daughter because that is who you are. Keep your vision and dreams in front of you, and don't get weary of reminding yourself who you are and of the royal rules. Seek a brighter way to manage your royal day. John Bytheway once said, "Inch by inch life's a cinch, yard by yard life is hard," and he couldn't have been more accurate. Make small changes and let the King of glory shine through.

YOU'RE SPECIAL

The phrase "you're special" has a unique meaning in our family. If one of my girls said that phrase, it really meant you did something not so smart. Like the time one of them announced she knew what 24/7 meant. "Oh," she said, "now I get it. I never knew it meant all weeks!" Or the time we were talking about genes, as in DNA, and one declared her jeans were too tight. Yes, I had many laughs with my three girls and lots of special moments. As a mother, I wanted my children to embrace their gifts because all three of them have different talents.

To stand out to be a sunflower is difficult, and declaring our gifts and talents might seem prideful. But consider the story of the man who buried his talents in Luke 19:22. What happened? "You wicked servant," the master declared. Why such hard words? I love it when someone is thankful for a gift. Can you think of gifting a friend their favorite flowers? How would you feel if they hid it away, acting as if they had not received it? Grow to develop that dream, whatever has been placed in your heart. You may not see how it will come to pass but don't hide your talents away. Do not shy away from His glory and what makes you special. Stand in it.

STANDING IN OUR DREAMS

How do you stand on a dream, grow your talents, or help your vision come to pass? You do it by taking one small step at a time. I have seen my dreams come true.

I've witnessed a vision become a reality. When I was young, I knew I wanted to design homes and make places beautiful, but I did not know the time and cost of making this a reality in my life. I just took one step at a time. Many were missteps and some costly mistakes, but I learned and grew through each experience. When I needed information or that perfect furniture or fabric, there it would be. Always pray for wisdom and direction.

Learning how to design window treatments is not easy. Even if you take a class, it will be nothing like reality. With fabric, one misstep can be very costly. In the early years of my design career, another designer took me under her wing to teach me. I was so grateful to learn all I could, but with few jobs and her limited time, I could not learn all I desired. We were working on a job together when I discovered one day that they had completed it without my knowledge. I thought she had stolen my client. But come to find out, it was the workroom fabricator who stole the client. I called our workroom to find out what happened, "How did these window treatments get fabricated and installed without me?" (I've learned to check things out, not jump to conclusions.) We had sent the fabricator to the client's home for some repair work on the first treatments, but she told the client to work with her directly.

Because of this stolen client, the main fabricator made me a deal because she didn't want to lose any more clients. She took me under her wing and taught me more about window treatment design than I could ever use. For a solid year, she showed up at every job, and I received one-on-

one instruction. What was bad was turned for my good. We waste nothing when we stand in our dreams. We still grow in the dark times. In my vision of writing *I Made the Rainbow*, I did not know the time it would take. I did not know if I could even write a book, let alone have anyone read it. God wants to birth dreams and visions in your life. I'm going to give you three ways that help you stand in your vision.

PRAY & PLAN

Prayer is essential for you to pursue your dreams. It seems simple. "Do not worry about anything, but pray about everything. With thankful hearts, offer your prayers and request to God. Then, because you belong to Christ Jesus, God will bless you with peace that no one completely understands. And this peace will control the way you think and feel" (Philippians 4:6–7, CEV).

Next, use what is in your hand, and *do* what you can. This is simple. "What is in your hand, Moses?" (Exodus 4:2, NIV). "Let the favor of the Lord our God be upon us, And establish the work of our hands upon us; Yes, establish the work of our hands" (Psalm 90:17, NKJV). Ask yourself, "What is in my hands for today?"

I see women chasing dreams with lots of activity that produces nothing. You cannot neglect what is on your plate today. Your dreams are like a lovely fabric added to your décor. The dream will complement your life, and you can't neglect one calling for another. If you have small children, then realize motherhood is a very important calling. Small children can't parent themselves. Someone must manage the home, and chores must be done. Do not be misled by saying, "My calling is greater; I'm not doing those dishes!" See the value in the smallest of jobs, the little things placed in our hands. I could have thought some of my early design jobs were too small and not at the level I dreamt of, but I did the minor jobs with excellence.

Last, you need a plan. Plan time and space for the dream, the vision, and for seeking wisdom. Use that calendar and schedule time. When working on my book, I would write late at night, and then sometimes, I would wake up at 4 a.m. to continue writing. I would design those "B-days" that were all about the book or have a half-B-day planned, but I always looked at my life and planned time for projects, writing, designing, work, family, and fun. All the petals of my sunflower came together to make my beautiful flower.

Your calling will not overtake you. We all know stories of pastors who lost their families because they didn't understand the call is only a part of who they are. I believe God will not place more on us than we can handle. I did not know that at sixty, I would publish my first book, and I had no idea while writing the first book that there would be a second. The timing was perfect because my season had changed. My children are grown, and I have time to stand in this calling.

God asked Moses to use what was in his hand. So now I ask you, "What do you have available right now? What is in your hand today?" Stand tall and own your dreams.

Don't be moved from that bright light called vision. "Arise, shine, for your light has come, and the glory of the Lord rises upon you" (Isaiah 60:1, NIV). Stand tall, firm, and strong, and let your light shine brightly!

CHAPTER FIVE:

THE SOIL

"Planted in the house of the Lord, they shall flourish in the courts of our God" (Psalm 92:13, KJV).

When I was six, in Freeport, Texas, I started out attending Sunday school and going to church with my family. Later, Dad started his own church after we moved to Rushville, Ohio. One Sunday morning, Daddy was preaching his salvation message with his hair combed like Elvis, wearing his black suit, white shirt, and black tie. He lifted his voice and his Bible, shaking it in the air! My seat was always front and center of the pulpit, so he could monitor me—sad to say, it was needed. Mama played the piano and sat on the platform.

There we were, my friend Lisa and I, giggling through our whispers, not giving a mind to Daddy's sermon. The windows of the old church were wide open on that spring day, and in flew a wasp. I don't know why it picked me, but it flew right up my skirt and stung me. I had a quick call to attention and a painful sting on my leg. I cried. As my tears fell, my dad stopped mid-sentence. He looked down at me and declared to the entire congregation that I should stop crying because I got what I deserved for talking in church! For years, I thought the Holy Spirit had sent that wasp to shut me up, and I had no trouble keeping quiet in future church services.

Since then, I have been a member of a few churches where I've been planted and felt at home. Anyone who has been a part of a church body knows it comes with people issues. We have gone through a few church splits, but one left us lost and discouraged. Terry and I were young and not very seasoned or rooted in our spiritual journey. We had met, married, and had our baby girls dedicated at this church. In my heart, I wanted to attend this church until the end of time. But it did not stand. Sadly, half the church burnt to the ground.

Our spiritual footing was gone, and we left feeling like desert wanderers. We did not wander to other churches, mind you; we stopped going altogether. We joined the many spiritually wounded warriors who would never dart into a church house again. Those people hurt us; those people let us down, and those church people—*who do they think they are?* They are people, just people. Then a little boy at our daughter's daycare died tragically. After attending his sad funeral, I left heavy-hearted and went home to tell Terry my fears, my what if, where would, and how would we cope with no pastor, no spiritual family to support us if tragedy came? We needed a church family. The Bible directs us to come together. I wanted a church home but didn't know where we should go. How would we feel safe?

The next Sunday, we visited a church. All dressed up, I directed each of my three girls to their Sunday school classes. At the last class, I dropped off my youngest daughter when a sweet mom with the most adorable little boy looked up and said, "Hello."

I said, "Hi."

"Are you new?" the mom asked.

"Yes!" I declared over the roaring noise of kids.

She put out her hand and said, "I'm Merlyn."

I replied, "I'm Deb." Then off to service, we went.

The next Sunday, rushing down the Sunday school hallway, I heard, "Hi, Betsy," over the roar of kids. Looking up, I saw Merlyn. "Oh, hi, Merlyn." But in my mind, I was thinking, *How did she get Betsy out of Deb? I need to let her know she has my name wrong.* But in a moment of rush, I let it go. The next Sunday, I decided I needed to tell Merlyn she had my name wrong. As I walked in, I heard, "Hey, Betsy, sorry I have to go. My son is not feeling well. Are you attending the ladies' meeting this evening?"

"Oh, well, yes, I plan to. I am so sorry, Merlyn. Hope he feels better soon."

I could hardly focus on the service. How had I let it go this far? That evening, I arrived at the women's event with one thought in mind to straighten out my name with

Merlyn once and for all. As I came into the room, set with flowers and teapots, I heard the name Betsy from across the room. She had kindly saved a seat for me. How kind, but the moment had come to correct her, and so as I sat down, I looked at her and said, "Merlyn, I'm just so sorry, but you have my name wrong. My name is not Betsy; it's Deb." She looked at me and laughed—not the response I expected. She was not embarrassed or shocked. She said, "I have been wanting to tell you my name is Denise, by the way!"

HOLY GROUND

In the Bible, many times, soil represents the importance of where we are planted. Rich soil brings forth the best produce, provides many trace minerals, and holds in moisture. In our journey to be a sunflower, we want to be planted in the richest soil possible, with a good fertilizer for our soil. Agriculture productivity is based on the correct feeding of nutrients. Without this feeding, the soil would become depleted and impoverished. (This sounds like some of us at times.) Jesus is our Gardener, and He directs our steps. A good church is a blessed connection to other believers, but it should also be the planting ground for the lost. A local church is a place that receives the lost and broken and has outreach.

Regarding church, I thought I should like everything that was served—all the fertilizer. Have you found a restaurant where you liked everything on the menu? But the church is not about us; it is about others. There will always be issues, and people will mess up, but do not allow people to keep you from the family of God, getting fed, and the blessing of worshiping together. Be planted deeply in that holy ground.

JOY IN PLENTY

The kind of soil we are planted in depends on our choices. "He who tills his land will have plenty of food, but he who follows empty pursuits will have poverty in plenty" (Proverbs 28:19, NIV). Times of favor and plenty have come my way, but due to wrong choices, I didn't have joy, abundance, or peace. I had a blessing without enjoyment. We must dig deep into our soil and uproot areas that can't supply soul food.

Terry and I now understand the value of being planted in a local church. We love our church and feel planted deep in the rich soil that it provides. We would love for our children to all be in one church home. But in honoring God's direction in their lives, they don't go the way Mom and Dad always want. We attended church with one of our daughters and her husband. Terry was always saying they were not plugged in; it seemed they were just attending with no joy in the soil, and the day came when they told us they were joining another church. We were heartbroken and didn't understand the reasons behind the change. But the soil at that other church started feeding their soul, and I witnessed my sweet girl grow spiritually. She was truly planted, and the fruit showed up. By leading a home group and volunteering, they developed spiritual maturity and found joy.

WHAT MAKES UP SOIL?

The particles that make up soil are in three categories: sand, silt, and clay. Soil can be all sand, all clay, or all silt. This, however, is rare; most soil is a combination of two or three. A mixture of soils has what is called trace minerals, rock, and organic matter. Soil is only as rich as the deposits that make up the soil. California's great central valley has some of the richest soil in the USA. With a Mediterranean climate, they grow over 230 different fruits and vegetables worth forty-six billion annually. That is some kind of soil. Rich soil is important when selecting a home church because good soil brings forth many fruits and lots of growth.

Making soil deposits takes care and effort. The farmer adds to the soil when needed. He knows the crop depends on the soil. He may pay the price and purchase the needed fertilizer or take waste from decayed plants and animals to add to his soil. We make deposits in our churches when we give, support, host a home group, mentor a young person, or pray for the sick. Some people may share their gifts of singing and songwriting. The church is only as good as the deposits made in it. What are you depositing?

DUSTY WORK

"The Lord God formed man from the dust of the ground and breathed into his nostrils the breath of life..." (Genesis 2:7, NIV). The Hebrew word for "dust" also means "clay."

This message came to Jeremiah from the Lord: "Jeremiah, go down to the potter's house. I will give you a message there." So I went down to the potter house and saw him working with the clay at the wheel. He was making a pot from clay. But something was wrong with the pot. So the potter used that clay to make another pot. With his hands, he shaped the pot the way he wanted it to be.

Jeremiah 18:1–4 (ERV)

The Potter, no matter the wrongs we have done or the flaws we have, can transform and reshape us. We all want to be a perfect pot, but perfection is like an infection and isn't healthy. Perfectionism can make us nonproductive. If we are critical, always self-evaluating, want everything to be perfect, or are overly concerned with others' opinions, then we may struggle with perfectionism. Perfectionists tend to spot mistakes and have trouble seeing anything else. We can unknowingly allow perfectionism to block our productivity, and it will stop us from acting on our dreams.

THE TEACHER

There was a ceramics teacher who put perfectionism to the test. He divided his class into two groups that would be graded differently. Group one would be graded on the quantity of the pots they produced, and group two would be graded on the quality of the pots they produced. They each had to create one near-perfect pot. At the end of the experiment, he evaluated the quality of the pots. The pots from group one, which focused on quantity, had higher quality than those from group two, which focused on "that one perfect pot." Turns out, the "doing" made them better. "Just do it quietly and unobtrusively. That is the way your God who conceived you in love, working behind the scenes" (Matthew 6:4, MSG).

RESTING THE SOIL

At sixteen, my family moved from Ohio back to Texas. My dad wanted to become a Texas oilman. He purchased an oilfield from a true Texas oilman, a gentleman with a cowboy hat and boots. I remember his large belt buckle had an oil well design on it. He had wisdom and knew the Texas oil business well. The day he sold the oil lease to my father, he explained he rested the wells for one day each week. The man told Dad to do whatever he wanted, but he felt rest made them produce more. As the man walked away, my dad had a big laugh, looked at my brothers, and said, "How do oil wells know what day it is? We are going to get more oil because we are going to pump seven days a week. We will produce more oil than he ever did." Did you know my dad's wells never produced as many barrels of oil as the rested oil wells produced?

"But during the seventh year, let the land rest unplowed and unused. Then the poor among your people may get food from it, and wild animals may eat what is left. Do the same with your vineyard and olive grove" (Exodus 23:11, NIV).

I think that in our 24/7 hurried lives, we need rest. We need to rest our bodies, and our families need to know how to rest. We need to rest from the media and learn how to quiet our hearts and minds. This is a lifestyle, not a vacation. Learn the simple idea of letting it go and taking a day each week to rest. Some can only rest if they are on vacation, but learning to rest in our homes is key. Then you will have more oil for your lamp, and your light will shine.

Pastor Robert Morris's book *Take the Day Off*[6] states it is not what you do; it's about what you don't do. Do not work! In my first book, *I Made the Rainbow*, I share how to have designer days. A day of rest might be a walk in the park, reading something that feeds the soul, music, or fun. If tennis refreshes you, go for it. Like the soil that was rested, the rest of your week will be more productive.

SOIL TEST

"But the fruit of the Spirit is love, joy, peace, patience, kindness, goodness, faithfulness, gentleness, self-control. Against such, there is no law" (Galatians 5:22–23, NKJV). You can tell which is good soil by what it produces. We won a cruise in the early '80s, and it was a trip to remember. The staff was attentive, and the food was delicious, but I was four months pregnant with our middle daughter and not feeling the best. I could not eat many of the foods, and the movement of the ship did not help. But I had food cravings, and I felt like I was starving. Having lost my dinner the evening before, I would wake so hungry.

The strangest combinations of foods appealed to me. Tomatoes and bananas stayed down, so I would find baskets of bananas and want to eat them all. A bowl of tomatoes made me so happy at lunchtime. The bananas were small, and they had a taste unlike any I had eaten. The ship picked them up from one of the islands, and they had ripened on the tree. The tomatoes also had a sweetness to them. Only on the ship did I desire to eat this way. The rich island soil produced amazing fruit. After growing in rich soil, the bananas and tomatoes had a special taste and smelled delicious. "Taste and see that the Lord is good" (Psalm 34:8, NIV). God invites you to the banquet to try the goodness of our great God.

LET'S DIG

How rich is your soil (church)? Do you feel planted by the almighty Gardener? The story Jesus tells in Matthew Chapter 13 is about the farmer who went out to plant, but the seeds fell on four different soils. In our home, where we raised our family, we had a garden with a sunken patio. We worked to make it lovely. We planted many flowers in this garden, but we discovered that the clay soil was hard to work with. It was rocky and hard to dig into. The large chunks of hard clay would stick to the shovels, and it took great effort to break up the soil. But we dug and dug, adding good soil where we planted mulch and fertilizer.

Over time, the ground became easy to dig, the plants easy to grow, and our garden flourished. The weeds pulled out with ease, and flowering plants bloomed in abundance—all due to the change in the soil. Lots of deposits over twenty-five years had produced the most beautiful garden. Terry spent hours making that garden a place of delight for me. The plants grew over the sidewalls, and the path was lined with all kinds of blooming plants. I witnessed and enjoyed the harvest, but I also witnessed the labor. Sunflowers can grow in any kind of soil because they are remarkably hardy, but they need full sunshine to thrive. You are hardy, and you can grow wherever there is "*Son*shine" and good soil!

CHAPTER SIX:

ROOTS

"And now, just as you accepted Christ Jesus as your Lord, you must continue to follow him. Let your roots grow down into him, and let your lives be built on him. Then your faith will grow strong in the truth you were taught, and you will overflow with thankfulness" (Colossians 2:6–7, NLT).

Roots love dirt. When my oldest daughter, Terah, was a toddler, if she got a speck of dirt on her tiny little hand, the meltdown would begin. She would come running, tears streaming down her little cheeks, showing Mommy that dot of dirt. Her younger sister, Taneia, was just the opposite. She loved dirt. She would play in whatever pile she could find, diaper off, as she rolled in the stuff. She even ate dirt a few times.

I was so blessed to have my two girls during that season of my life. The second week after Taneia was born, I felt like I had stayed home long enough, and I could not ignore the call of the mall. No one had time to go with me, but

I had to get out of the house. With a new stroller to try, I dressed my darling baby girls all in pink—hair bows, cute dresses with lace socks, nothing less would do.

As we drove into the mall parking lot, joy filled my mind, and the excitement of shopping filled my heart. The thought that I now had lifelong shopping buddies was exciting. Terah was close to three, and as I removed her from the car seat, I heard a sound, the sound that tells you baby needs changing badly, and right now! *I got this*, I thought, *I can manage two little girls*, so with the car door open, I laid the baby in the front seat. Since Terah was out of the car, I placed her in front of me. This way, she could not run off into the parking lot. With my sweet little girl between the baby and me, I began to change the diaper.

As I was lifting her baby sister's legs to place her bottom in the clean diaper, there was a perfectly timed blowout. Poop landed right on the center of Terah's forehead, and then two perfect plops landed on her pretty pink dress. I looked down, knowing I had maybe fifteen seconds before the meltdown began. I worked fast to clean up the baby and get that diaper on. I watched as my toddler's face changed expression and color as she realized she had poop on her little pink dress. As she wailed, I quickly removed her dress. In the parking lot with a crying baby and screaming naked toddler, I realized my defeat, and the only place I wanted to be at that moment was home. There I went, and there I stayed for many weeks. You could say I became rooted and grounded at home.

AMAZING ROOTS

Roots grow in the most amazing places, through rocks and concrete, and on the sides of mountains, through all kinds of cracks and crevasses. Roots can break apart foundations when left unchecked, causing significant damage. I remember pulling the old plants from Grandma Anna's garden. After the plant produced their food, Grandma would pull them right up and out of the garden, tossing them aside. It was easy. They had not been growing very long and could only produce one season.

Out, they would pop. I helped her most mornings when the soil was soft and moist. I've pulled up older roots that took hours of digging, cutting, and digging more to free a mature root system. We took out a large tree where the root system was going to damage our home's foundation. They filled two truckloads with roots only. Like plants, we must grow where we can develop the best root system. The deeper, the better, I say. But pulling out any roots that have caused damage in your life can be painful and takes time, depending on how long and deep they are. "Follow peace with all men, and holiness, without which no man shall see the Lord: Looking diligently lest any root of bitterness springing up trouble you, and thereby many be defiled" (Hebrews 12:14–15, KJV).

Roots of hurt can damage your soul and cause harm to others. As Hebrews states, looking diligently, like good gardeners, we must keep an eye on what takes root in our hearts. The garden plants were easy to remove because they had not been in Grandma Anna's garden long, but the large tree in our yard, those roots had been there for twenty-five years. One took a quick jerk while the other took a truck with chains and a crew of men to remove. How long your heart has held that pain will matter to your healing journey. It may take a quick act of forgiveness or many hours of counseling and prayer to free your heart's garden of damaging roots. The key is to follow peace in direction and decisions. Let peace lead you into wholeness.

IN THE ZONE

Plants have zones. The zone is the area that gives the best environment for a healthy plant. In our state, Texas, we have four zones. Plants thrive in the correct zone. The Amazon rainforest is a perfect example. It is said to provide a habitat for over 40,000 plant species! Many of these plants can only grow in this forest with a perfectly humid tropical climate. The correct zone is everything for plant life. Have you tried to plant something in your garden that needed another zone? My sweet mamaw was always pulling plants from her Louisiana yard as she handed me a handful of green. "Here. Stick this in the ground; it will grow!" Many did not, but one plant went crazy, and it grew better in my garden than hers. She was amazed. It had found the right zone and loved the amount of Texas sunshine and rain it received.

In Texas, we are blessed with our lovely state flower, the bluebonnet. Bluebonnets are everywhere in the spring. They magically pop up along the roadsides, with large fields filled with waves of blue. We even have a bluebonnet trail where folks flock to see their beauty each year, and there is a bluebonnet festival held around the middle of April in Burnet, Texas. This season is a great photo opportunity. I have many photos of my girls and grandbabies. It is a Texas tradition. Texas has a zone that is perfect for bluebonnets. They are at home here, and they flourish.

YOUR ZONE

You have a home zone, and finding the zone will make for deep, mature roots. Some people use the term "comfort zone," but God's zone may not fit that term for your life. To have deep roots in Him, you may need your roots to grow out of their comfort zone. We are part of a life group and, over the years, have been involved in many groups. Small groups grow relational roots, and we all need that kind of connection.

The life group we are a part of today was not initially in my comfort zone, but I knew God planted us in this group. Terry and I have been meeting with this group for a few years now, and it feels comfortable in this season, but in the beginning, not so much. We seemed to have little in common with the members. We are the youngest couple, and most of the members have a high level of success and speak multiple languages and teach in other countries. Many have ministries and have written many books—more success than I can dream of. However, I have grown so much by being a part of this mature group of Christians and seeing their deep roots. My heavenly Gardener, with

His lovingkindness, placed me there to grow. And grow, I have, taking in the spiritual richness. I thrive in this zone.

SUNFLOWER ROOTS

The roots of the sunflower change the soil. When the mature flower dies, it leaves behind its root system, and the soil is changed for the better. The soil now holds more moisture because of the roots deposited by the sunflower. This aids the other plants left behind. Now, they can grow better and thrive because of the root deposit the departed sunflower left. Maybe you had a year of "no comfort zone" that brought great growth. I walked through such a year with the loss of a dear friend, Debra.

I met Debra on a girls' trip. My friend of many years, Karol, planned a trip with three of her dear friends, along with her twin sister, Karen. We planned to meet in Dallas and, from there, travel across Texas. I wasn't in my comfort zone, though, because these were Karol's friends. I knew her sister but not the two other ladies. Karol assured me I would love them both. She explained, "Tammy is from Florida and fun-loving. She works in the travel industry. And Debra is the sweetest person you could ever know. She owns a pizza place and works alongside her husband. She has a lovely family and is grandma to three grandsons. Deb, you are going to love her." Karol explained to me that Debra had dealt with cancer three times, and she had just recovered from a hard treatment on her liver but was doing great. The doctors were giving her a good report—all clear, no cancer.

We drove to meet Debra at the local Lexus dealership. She was standing in front of this shiny red car, hair blowing in the wind with gifts for us all and donuts. She was ready to start the fun! I liked Debra and Tammy instantly and knew I was in for a great time. We had a few lovely Texas days together, going to Waco to see Magnolia Market and then visiting friends in Chico. We said goodbye, named ourselves "the journey girls," and went on our way.

The holidays came, and we all stayed in touch. Debra was coming into town, and we made plans to spend the day together. When I saw her, I knew instantly things were not right. She felt sick in her stomach all the time and could not eat much. I prayed with her as we said goodbyes. Then I started waking up every morning with her in my heart, so I prayed. Most times, 4 a.m. was the call to prayer, and many times, she would be awakened at 4 a.m. as well. I would encourage her, but mostly she encouraged me. Never did she complain. In fact, it was hard to find out how she was doing. The journey girls were there for her, and we would be the shoulders to uphold her and pray for her. We would pray, and she would get better. She could leave the ICU and return home. The treatment had worked against cancer, but her liver was failing. Eventually, she was in and out of the hospital, mostly in with drains and doctors making every attempt to save her.

I went to visit her in the Tyler Hospital. I felt so much hope that she would be okay, and I had faith this sweet friend would pull through. She had so much life in her eyes and a big smile. But as time went on, the battle was lost.

She went to bed talking with her husband one night, and the next day, she could not speak. They informed us she had maybe two weeks or fewer. I fell to my knees; how could this be? She was young and so beautiful.

During our short friendship, I was grateful for her kindness. I was grateful God had placed me in her life and that I had been there for her, but then I heard that still, small voice, "No, no, baby girl." (God calls me baby girl. I just hear Him that way, especially when He wants to teach me something.) "I placed her in *your* life." As the flood of memories hit my heart, I realized the growth in my walk through this year. I was reading my Bible more, and my prayer times had changed too. At the hospital, unable to speak, she had visitors who played music and sang. When all of a sudden, they realized Debra was singing, they stopped to hear her singing every word perfectly. Eventually, she passed away.

I received a call about her service and was informed that she had planned her funeral. I was listed in her friends' choir. Right there in her Bible was my name. There was a little problem: I do not sing. The choir consisted of her friends who were there for her through the many years of sickness and the birth of her children—who was I to receive such honor? *Why me?* I thought. What a true friendship blessing and what a deposit. I spoke that day about the roots of a sunflower. Debra was a true sunflower, a gift to all who knew her. How many have left roots in your life that changed you? I know we all have sunflower deposits in our hearts. Many deposits have come from the pain we receive through loss; deposits are the legacy we leave behind.

FAMILY ROOTS

As I write this book, our country shares the sad loss of a former first lady, Barbara Bush. I was a fan, admiring her wit, confidence, and values. The White House and public life were not the first lady's idea of living in her comfort zone. But she grew where she was planted. Barbara was a star, and she shone brightly, surrounded by other bright lights. She knew who she was. She felt confident about being true to herself and living a life of joy.

Losing a little daughter could have become her center, and sadness could have defined her life, but faith gave her the courage to live in the center and enjoy her life. With deep faith, strong love for family, and a passion for children to read, she put down deep roots. I love the fact she wore fake pearls to conceal wrinkles on her neck and kept her natural color hair so she could enjoy playing golf, tennis, and swimming. She knew her zone and found her comfort in it. In an interview, she shared these facts with her granddaughter. She decided not to fit the mold others may have wanted to place her in. I admire her for what she did, but I also admire her for what she did not do.

DEEP ROOTS

It is said of Mrs. Bush that she would come into an interview and give them five minutes of her time knowing what she wanted to say. She valued herself and her time. She had grace and did not feel the need to impress everybody. Pretend you are in an interview, and I ask you, "Please list ten things you don't do." Maybe you don't eat sweets or spend only fifteen minutes a day on social media. You refuse to gossip, and you will never miss your daily workout. You never allow self-pity or negative self-talk to consume your mind. The "don't dos" are of great value and can become a strong root system in your life and family, affecting those around you. We see this example in Mrs. Bush's children and grandchildren. She leaves behind a quality character and legacy for many generations.

As I start a New Year, I always make resolutions or want-to-dos like losing weight, reading more, and saving more. This year, make some "don't do" resolutions. What if you list anything that would place you off-center? Don't allow people to rob your time ticks, and view time with value and care. What would your list of "don't dos" look like?

Roots is my favorite coffee shop. I love the name and coffee. My granddaughters and I make hot cocoa there. I am putting down roots by spending time talking and sharing with them. Deep roots come your way when you spend time with your heavenly Father. Sink deeply into His lovingkindness and grow. "Let your roots grow down into him, and let your lives be built on him. Then your faith will grow strong in the truth you were taught, and you will overflow with thankfulness" (Colossians 2:7, NLT). "Therefore, my beloved brethren, be steadfast, immovable, always abounding in the work of the Lord, knowing that your labor is not in vain in the Lord" (1 Corinthians 15:58, NKJV).

LET'S DIG

Roots represent legacy and intentionality. We all have roots, but where we plant them is our choice. In this season of my life, I'm choosing to plant my roots and spread my legacy through time with my grandchildren. My roots remain healthy because I've planted them in the good soil of my local church, where I'm involved in the community and relational care.

Ephesians 3:17 (NLT) reads, "Then Christ will make His home in your hearts as you trust in Him. Your roots will grow down into God's love and keep you strong." Christ dwells in our hearts through faith so we can be rooted and anchored by His great love. Love is our roots. It takes work to uproot old habits, and it takes love to put down new roots of faith. According to the dictionary definition, roots are usually the underground part of the seed and function as an organ of absorption in food storage and support of sorts that is different from the stem. In other words, the roots act as an anchor and a food line for the plant—vital for its survival. In the same way, our spiritual roots are vital for our spiritual growth and health.

Take a minute and think about your roots. Are they planted in healthy soil? Are you using them to help nourish others and your legacy? If not, then intentionally plant yourself where you will best grow and where you can help others grow as well. When our roots go deep with intention, we will produce lasting fruit that will nourish others in the same way my friend Debra's life nourished me and many others. Let your roots go deep in God's Word, and in healthy relationships, watch the growth that will happen!

CHAPTER SEVEN:
SUNFLOWER FIELDS

Lights of golden tumbling to bloom.

In full glory of sunshine moving to tune.

Bold beauty's rising so tall.

Then growth though the darkness, they wake one and all.

Surrounded by many, the blooms they compose.

Sunflower magic, a sight to behold.

"Golden's Beauty"

Sunflowers may look the same, but no two are identical. They have the same needs to devote to sunlight, obtain water, and have their roots deeply planted. They need good soil to stand tall in. We have many examples of women with a sunflower-like faith all around us. I've enjoyed the ministries of Joyce Meyer, Beth Moore, Christine Caine, Victoria Osteen, and my sweet pastor's wife, Debbie Morris. Beth Moore's Bible studies changed me, adding great richness to my soul. I enjoyed three studies through my church, and then I led one in a friend's home. I got my group together and wanted it to be as "Beth-like" as possible. I copied the scriptures and turned them into bookmarkers. We had our coffees and Bibles in hand, and every week, we came together and learned about Daniel.

Beth knew how to make it fun by sharing stories of real events in her life. I wanted my group to feel as if Beth were right there with us. Beth had shared a story about a spray tan; I had never tried a spray tan booth but thought, *Well, we don't have Beth, but I can have a Beth-like experience.* So off to the tanning place I went. (I need to note here I have a bit more real estate than Beth.) I got in the booth, and it sprayed as I turned around, and when I walked out, I was pleased with the nice tan shade it left on my skin. I could not wait to tell my girls the next day.

As I prepared for our study the next morning, I wore my capris pants and did my Texas hair, just like Beth, and I was ready to walk out the door. I had that week's scriptures all laminated for my girls, my big bag, and my Bible. As I took one last look in the mirror, I noticed some stripes running down the back of my legs. Oh, no! They were dark, and I had about three on each leg. I reached for the nail polish remover and then thought, *Better to use soap and water first,* so I did. Then, I reached for the nail polish remover. But nothing was lightening the stain. The Bible study had to go on. I shared it with the girls, and we had a good laugh. That was many years ago. Now I know I can be me. My gifts are all God needs to fulfill His plan in my life. I've not had a spray tan since, though.

There are women who are called to lead and women who are called to follow and support. Each calling is important. I know many women are called to lead, but most of us have a natural ability to follow. It's challenging to know how to lead and display our talents without looking proud. I see many women with amazing talents that you practically have to pull out of them. They hide in fear of shining too brightly. There is great risk in coming out to the sunlight— letting others know this is what the King gave you. I've been given gifts and ashamed.

INTENTIONAL LIVING

My eighth-grade teacher called me "money bags" because my dad had a large motor home business and was on television. Everyone thought we were very wealthy, and yes, Daddy was successful. We had nice cars and motor homes, but I wanted to be like everybody. Daddy was a gift-giver, and he would buy many things for me, wanting his little girl to have what he had never had. But I hid it away, and I would never tell my friends. They teased me when I got a brand-new car, and I didn't like the teacher calling me "money bags."

I remember a boy I so wanted to date who was from a poor family, but he wouldn't speak to me because he thought I was well off. If I could go back with the view I have now, how different would my heart be toward my father? I would have a receiving heart. After I wrote *I Made the Rainbow*, the praise and wonderful feedback from so many were overwhelming. Hearing how it had blessed and changed homes made my heart glad. But I was not in my comfort zone.

I had to live intently, accepting and owning the gift God had given. I'm barely on social media because what do you want me to post to followers? And pray tell, what do I say? I learned to be a sunflower and to reach for the gift, hold it up, and say, "Thank You, thank You, Father. I'm blessed and will tell everyone who will listen about Your rainbow and how You want to shine and show off in Your daughters' homes and lives. How You want them to be sunflowers for You, full of love beams that bounce off to others." We must live with intent.

My Terry has a favorite restaurant in Fort Worth, Joe T. Garcia's, and we can be found there once a week, mostly on Thursday evenings. For about four years, we have been treating friends and family to dinner or lunch. Reaching out to old friends and trying to invite new ones. At least once at every meal, our guests will say, "Now, next time, we are taking you guys out." After two, maybe three times, they say, "We will call you, and it's our treat." Did you know I can only count five times we have been treated to dinner by our friends? It's not that they don't want to, nor is it they don't care; it is simply that they don't live with intention.

Intentional living means you deliberately decide based on your values and beliefs.

Here is Deb's way: have a plan, make it simple, and

work the plan. Every year, I plan to start a workout routine, but somehow, I don't get there. I get discouraged because I don't know what exercise I want to do, walking, weights, or swimming? There are too many selections. Then I wonder what I should wear. I lack a plan. In years past, when planning, I was up every day to spend two hours exercising. You get it; not simple, so I never made it to number three—working the plan. This year, I planned a couple of evenings to walk around my neighborhood; the plan is simple, and the plan is workable.

THE SUNFLOWER'S FIELD

Sunflower fields are amazing to see in bloom, the great golden flowers standing tall all together. The pollen from one helps to feed and grow the other sunflowers. Friends feed our souls and add growth. We receive great blessings from rich relationships, but did you know you cannot make an old friend? We must cultivate old friendships over many years. As I grow older, I have prioritized my relationships. I value my friends more now than ever.

In this age of social media, we place too much value on how many online friends you have or who is following you on Twitter. But social networking is not a replacement for face-to-face friendship. The field of friendship helps us stand tall, making us look good. A lone sunflower is not as stunning as a field of sunflowers. The sunflower placed in a field of many with their golden heads joined all together brings greater glory and beauty.

A friend of mine sadly shared that her children were pulling away. She said, "I thought we would be this close family, always wanting to do things together. But it's not happening the way I thought it would." I see my grandbabies growing and getting more involved with their friends. Grammie is not the bright star in their world that I once was.

The desire is normal to have expectations that this family unit that once was so close would always want to get together. How can these children I birthed into this world not want to spend more time with me? The truth is that kids grow and go—just a fact. As parents, we will not always be invited to be a part of everything, nor will our kids always want to hang out with us. Terry and I got a lot more visit time when we were the babysitters, but the calls and visits are less and less as their lives become full and the grandchildren become more social. It is okay. I don't want to make you sad. I'm just sharing so you can understand the value of tending to that friendship field.

FIELD OF DREAMS

I tell young moms, moms of teens, and moms with adult children, that once you have children, many issues come along with the blessings. I refer to children as blessed burdens. Moms say to me, "Will they grow out of this?"—like a magic fairy is going to come down and touch your sweet baby, then they will not make a mess, throw fits, then they will keep their room tidy and honor all house rules. This will not happen; that is a sweet dream. Children need a field, a group of people who care about them, and they need a field with high fences.

This may not be popular advice, but let me share. If it's an issue with a baby, find a daycare, if only for a day each week. Get help because you need a break, if only a short one. For an issue with a toddler, hire a nanny; for issues with a teen, get a mediator; for issues with adult children, let it go and allow them the privilege of figuring it out!

The daycare can give you some air and the baby some needed playtime and structure. The nanny, if only for a week, will change your home and add rules that you never knew were needed, so take notes. And the mediator for a teen who has lost all honor for you will make the house rules clear and the consequences even clearer. I had a nanny at times growing up, and I loved how they added structure to our home. I received help from all three areas. The best advice is to get help. Do not feel you have to handle everything alone because you are the mother. Find a moms' group or an older mother to guide you in the seasons of child-rearing. With time, they will grow, and your dream will become a reality.

FIELD MANAGEMENT

I book dates with friends on my calendar, and I like to have them over at my home. I learned to make good coffee and throw together a quick salad. Omelets are easy because you can talk and make them at the same time. In my home, we can hear each other and talk freely. Unlike a restaurant, I enjoy the connection of dining in. It's much more personal, and if your friend needs prayer or to shed a tear, the home is best. I encourage you to invite your friends to your table and add to your field.

I ask this question when I talk with women, "Do you have a friend date on your calendar right now?" When was the last time you had friend time, not phone time, but face-to-face fun? In a field of sunflowers, as you allow the roots to die off, the water-holding capacity increases over time, giving your garden the ability to withstand drought conditions. Friends can help you stand through hard seasons as well. Some friends come into your life for a season and a reason, then move away, and some simply go by the way for no reason other than the changing of seasons. But all friends leave a deposit that will take you through many seasons to come—leaving behind a change in your field and adding to your bloom.

DESIGN THE FIELD

When starting a design project for a new building, we start out working with an architect. Many times, this process can go on for a year before they lay the foundation. The hours of planning and design work are the foundation for the great finish. It may not be as fun as the art and furnishing design, but the value of time and effort makes all the difference in the final project. There isn't much to see while clearing the ground and laying the foundation, but this is necessary for the builders to be successful.

Clearing your field of the past and creating a foundation to stand on takes time. Today, our issue is instant results, and we don't enjoy the journey. I can tell when a client has built something before because they are relaxed and they know the time and cost. However, someone who has never built a new home or worked with a designer doesn't understand the cost or the time needed to invest in the field. The Biltmore Estate, the largest home in America, took six years to complete. With 250 rooms, the workforce was around 1,000 laborers. When a home is built with care and time on a solid foundation, it can withstand the storms that come. Jesus told the parable of the wise and foolish builder to help us understand this principle:

> *Therefore, everyone who hears these words of mine and puts them into practice is like a wise man who built his house on the rocks. The rain came down, the stream rose, and the winds blew and beat against that house; yet it did not fall because it had its foundation on the rock. But everyone who hears these words of mine and does not put them into practice is like a foolish man who built his house on the sand. The rain came down, the streams rose, and the winds blew and beat against that house, and it fell with a great crash.*

Matthew 7:24–27 (NIV)

Today, many issues can tear down our homes. Build on the rock the stone that is eternal, Jesus.

FIELD OF BLESSINGS

I was blessed to live in the same neighborhood for almost twenty-five years, and the rich friendships and connections added great value to my life. I could ring the doorbell of a few of them anytime, day or night. But then we moved. I knew I needed to make new connections and have friendships nearby, but this was difficult for me. I prayed and, amazingly, made great new friendships. I made one new friendship due to mixed-up mail. I kept receiving mail from another home in our neighborhood, and I had to walk the mail to this neighboring home about three times, so I said, "Debbie, I think we should be friends." Well, Debbie is a dear friend to this day. Please get to know folks around the corner and up the street.

Today, we are more connected through social media; I do not think negatively about it at all. I can keep in touch with some far-away family members. But the facts show nothing beats face-to-face encounters. The relationships that grow us are lessening—replaced with lifestyles full of busyness. We are too rushed, too in a hurry to sit and visit. Texting is the preferred method of communication, quick and unemotional, and quilting circles and canning sessions are no longer a part of our society. I miss my old neighborhood friends who taught me hospitality and some great recipes. They added so much growth and beauty to my field!

WORKING THE FIELD

Early in my interior design business, my profit was small. I would work a design job and come out with little. But I had a neighbor who had built her business from the ground up, and she explained to me that as I realized my value and worth, I would come to understand my gift for designing spaces. When this happened, I would view my clients as receiving a valued service and not as someone paying me a fee. My talent, which I had been freely blessed with, was of great worth to others. I would then feel comfortable charging more, and the profit would come. Her relationship was so meaningful to me, and she added growth to my field. She was right! As I valued myself and understood my clients needed my talents, I learned to bill them based on the worth of my service. But gifts are hard to charge for at times. They were freely given to us, and it's so easy to give them away.

Another dear friend in the design business seemed to be working out of my comfort zone. She was working design jobs on a level I only dreamed of, and they voted her the top designer in the Dallas area. Why would she befriend me? But she did, and I would never have had the success I enjoy without her friendship. She even blessed me with a few design clients. The field you grow in is your choice, so select those who will add richness to your life. When you hang out with the negative down-and-outs (the weeds, so to speak), your growth is choked, and your dreams get trampled. You want friends who lift you higher, and you want to lift others up as well. "Therefore encourage one another and build one another up just as you are doing" (1 Thessalonians 5:11, ESV). What makes your field grow are the friends you reach out to with the purpose of adding value to their lives. Our fields should include young and old plants in wide colorful varieties.

LET'S DIG IN THE SOIL

Is it true we become like the friends we hang out with? Quickly, name three friends, your besties. Question: What makes them so? Why are they the best? My best friends pull me forward, and they are rich in faith. Time with them makes me feel lighter, and they aren't drama queens— only King's daughters. I have relationships for both encouragement and mentoring, and I think we all should. Examine your heart's needs and look around at the field of growth; what do you see? You are standing in how many sunflowers? What is in your field?

FREEDOM FIELDS

Your field needs to be free of weeds, and your environment needs space for life. Growth must have room. Like any garden, there will be weeds. All gardeners know a weed can pop up overnight. A good rain can bring growth and weeds. Life is full of unexpected storms, but our growth happens when we handle the storms with God's grace and truth. But when we wait to pull the weeds, they become harder to pull. The wise women in Proverbs 31:16 (NASB) say, "She considers a field and buys it; From her earnings, she plants a vineyard."

Okay, I'm not talking about perfection or spotless homes, but I see laziness robbing people of life-giving spaces. They just seem overwhelmed and unable to manage a home or life. Please give yourself grace here. However, failure and a lack of order in the home can rob you of joy. But there is hope. Reach out and find someone in your life gifted with the talent of organization. That friend that I made through the mail mix-up, Debbie, is blessed with organization, and she blessed me with her skill. I smile each time I open my pantry.

Ask for help, if only to have them mentor you. I've asked friends how to budget and their secret for keeping their home so lovely. Men find asking for direction hard, but women struggle to ask for help in the home. Clean up your field, and free your home from clutter and weeds. You cannot shine in the darkness among the clutter. Hire a cleaning service, if only once a month. You cannot do it all.

Get your house in order. I know young women today who have no joy in housekeeping and in an orderly home, not only no joy but no desire to have order. "Seek, and ye shall find," as the old King James Bible says. "So I say to you; ask, and it will be given to you; seek, and you will find; knock, and the door will be opened to you" (Luke 11:9, NIV). Pursue a better way, like the sunflowers that seek to keep going up, up out of the weeds.

FIELD OF WEEDS

My girls worked in the service industry, waiting tables. When they ran behind or had too many tables to serve, they would declare, "I'm in the weeds!" Have you been in the weeds? I recall a few weedy days. Many years back, I joined a volunteer group that raised funds to support needs in our community. I loved everything about this group: the social connections, the friendships, and the good causes we supported. But within the group, there was a power struggle, and the meetings were stressful. I would leave the meetings with a heavy heart because of the backbiting. The group was a case of 90 percent good, but the 10 percent that was bad was terrible.

One day, mid-meeting, the truth hit home, and I knew I was done. I gently spoke the truth and left. In doing so, I pulled some weeds. It took great bravery to leave, but I knew I had to go to another field. After I pulled up, others left, and the group dissolved. The Bible tells us to put our hands to the plow. "But Jesus said to him, 'No one, having put his hand to the plow, and looking back, is fit for the kingdom of God'" (Luke 9:62, NKJV). My dad would let me ride on the tractor. Behind, he pulled this large machine that looked like multiple giant pizza cutters, and it cleared the field weeds. No farmer would plant a field without first clearing the weeds. No growth can come if we hang out in a field full of weeds.

CHANGING FIELDS

Weeding your field is good, but sometimes you just have to change fields or friends. How many relationships do we cling to because we are too insecure to let go? I recently had a design appointment that left me stressed out. (It's hard to stress me these days.) I've had all kinds of clients and worked through many issues. This client was selecting fabrics for window treatments. She invited her friend to help with the selection. The client would love a fabric the friend would flat-out say she did not; then, my client would explain to her friend why she loved it. At one point, the friend told my client, "Well, I don't know what you want. I have no idea what you're going for." I tried to chime in with designer advice because I was the professional in the room, but her friend told me I was wrong and that he didn't like the texture of that fabric. The client made no selections, and the appointment was draining. Be brave, have faith, and trust in yourself. Move on to greener pastures. Change can be hard but so needed.

NO REGRETS

Once you have cleared your field of weeds, then keep moving forward and don't look back. When I think of someone who has not looked back, Kathie Lee Gifford comes to mind. I'm a fan of her wit. She is a bright light and a true sunflower. In her book *It's Never Too Late*,[7] she shared how she has moved from what many may have seen as a perfect setup to follow her path. She cleared many fields and embraced growth with great success. Her book opens with this poem:

I NEED TO MAKE A CHANGE IN MY LIFE

I need to make a change in my life.

To rearrange what's left of the rest of my life.

I've been living far too long in this dusty old room.

I need to plant a dream… I need to watch it bloom.

I need to make a choice in my life.

Surrender to the voice I've ignored all my life.

I've been waiting far too long, watching dreams pass me by.

I need to learn to live before I die.

I hunger to taste more while I still have the gift of time.

To taste a wine so sweet, I never dreamed it could be mine.

To savor every sunset and to say at the end of the ride.

I smiled at every sunrise; I sailed on every tide.

No question was unasked, no glance was ignored.

I drank deep from the well, more than I could afford.

I can't waste another chance, can't waste another day.

Watching all my dreams just waste away.

No regrets.

No what-ifs.

No if-onlys.

No what might have been.

I need to make a change in my life.[8]

CHAPTER EIGHT:

SUNSHINE

"A sunbeam, / a sunbeam / Jesus wants me for a sunbeam / a sunbeam, / a sunbeam, / I'll be a sunbeam for Him" ("Jesus Wants Me for a Sunbeam").[9]

Growing up, we sang "Jesus Wants Me for a Sunbeam" every Sunday. And it's true! Jesus wants to reflect His light through us. Our only goal is to be a "*Son*beam." God wants us to be a light for Him, living life reflectively. Sunbeams show up on a cloudy day and look like stripes of light flowing from the heavens and touching the earth. When viewing sunbeams peeking through clouds, I think of God Himself smiling on His creation. The darker the clouds, the brighter the beams become—a glory to behold. I love sunshine, and here in Texas, we have plenty. My front porch is the perfect place to sit in the rays of the sun. I love to sit in my comfy rocking chair, enjoying my flowers with a cup of tea or a great book. I love the sunshine and crave its warmth. I hope you have a sunny spot in your life that you can enjoy. Let your light shine before men and show off God's good work in you.

Seek Him in the morning with the Word like the sunflower seeks the sunrays; the mornings have meaning. "O God, You are my God; Early will I seek You; My soul thirst for You, My flesh longs for You In a dry and thirsty land, where no water is" (Psalm 63:1, NKJV).

We all have a favorite scripture, and Psalm 63:1 is mine. Most mornings, I wake with it in my heart. I want to stay thirsty. I want to desire Him. Many mornings, I wake up full, full of thoughts of myself, the day, my work, and all I am looking forward to. But then I remind myself that I do not want to be full—I want to be empty so that He can fill me.

Have you ever attended a dinner party, but since you had a late lunch meeting, you were already full? Even though the food was so good, you didn't get to enjoy what was available to you because you were too full. I desire to stay spiritually hungry, to stay seeking Him with my whole heart. "But seek ye first the kingdom of God and His righteousness, and all these things shall be added unto you" (Matthew 6:33, KJV).

SUNSHINE ROOM

Like the young sunflower, at the start of each new day, reset to the east and face the sunrise. "This is the day the Lord has made; we will rejoice and be glad in it" (Psalm 118:24, NKJV).

Sounds like a command; we will be glad, we will rejoice. It takes more than a strong mind to set your heart like a flint that no matter if your prayers are answered or not, you will rejoice. The hope of God is still working in us and through us. Be filled up with joy full of grace, and face each day with new hope in Him. Plan the end of the day so you can face the new day ahead with your heart set to receive God's love beams. In the evening, reflect on the little details of your day, and don't live from one big event to the next. Small, simple routines can bring great joy.

Make evenings the planning part of the new day. God started His creation in the evening. In Genesis, evening and morning were the first times. Planning your day the evening before allows you to wake in the morning with no thoughts, with the plan of the day all done. Then you can start your day with time in the Son. Do you have a sunshine room, a place to go and sit where you can be in the sunlight? Soak up some glory before your day starts. Do you have a place to end your day? Pen that plan, and plan for joy.

FACING THE SON

Soaking in the sun isn't just for the sunflowers. We need it too! Sunshine is essential for the health of humans and sunflowers alike. When we spend time in the sun, our bodies produce vitamin D. As little as fifteen minutes of sunshine a day is enough to give us the sun's health boost. And did you know that vitamin D is essential for your immune system by helping your body maintain calcium for strong bones, lowering your blood pressure, and promoting mental health? Those who miss out on the benefits of the sun are more prone to depression and a weaker immune system. By following the example of the sunflower and soaking in the sunshine, we will benefit mentally and physically. (But don't forget the sunscreen, especially if you are fair-skinned.)

Young sunflowers move their face to follow the sun. It's a beautiful sight to see a field of young flowers waking up facing east and moving throughout the day to the west at sunset. At nighttime, they reset their large blooms to face east as the sun's rays begin a new day. Also, when the flower matures, it sets itself east, and its overall growth slows down.

As young Christians, we need to follow Him day by day, sometimes hour by hour. In doing so, we reposition our hearts to get the best reflection of His glory. "Because the Sovereign Lord helped me. I will not be disgraced. Therefore have I set my face like a flint, and I know I will not be put to shame" (Isaiah 50:7, NIV). Flint is a well-known stone, a variety of quartz. It is extremely hard and used to strike a fire. I no longer have the temptation to steal, but sadly, there was a time when I did. As a teenager, I hung out in the wrong field, and I shoplifted on a dare but did not get caught. I felt the weight of my actions; how could I do something like that? Just because a friend said, "Put the earrings in your bag, I dare you!" I no longer have shame over this event, and grace covered my wrong. But no dare or desire, not even a little thought of taking something that did not belong to me, tempts me today. I am so grateful we did not get arrested as teenagers. Many struggles I had to overcome fell by the wayside as I followed the Son.

The struggle that everyone needs to like me and approve of me and that my children need to fit in my expectations and feelings of failure and disappointment are all gone. With a set heart comes great freedom. I am not perfect, let me get that straight, but I know my Redeemer lives, and I know He walks with me. My heavenly Father brings sunshine to shed light on each issue I face. My heart is strongly set, and I can face anything with Him. "For God, who said, 'Let light shine out of darkness,' made his light shine in our hearts to give us the light of the knowledge of God's glory displayed in the face of Christ" (2 Corinthians 4:6, NKJV).

Essentially, the older plants settle facing the east because it reflects more strongly the light early in the day. The older sunflowers are set, wanting to catch the first morning light. In this way, they attract insects and encourage pollination. I hope you are as excited at this picture of our journey as I am. Many believe there is significance to the Eastern Gate of Jerusalem (also called the Golden Gate or the Beautiful Gate), and many believe Jesus will return at the Eastern Gate. In Matthew 21, when Jesus entered Jerusalem from the Mount of Olives, he used a gate in the same location. The Eastern Gate has remained sealed for 500 years. "Set your mind on things above not on things on the earth" (Colossians 3:2, NKJV). We can celebrate aging with grace when we have our faces set on the Son, waiting for His return.

RAINY DAYS

No sunflower would put up an umbrella and say, "I do not need any sunshine today; I can live off the old sunshine from yesterday." In the same way, His mercies are new every morning. You can receive the gift of His righteousness; it is for all to receive. Just like that daily vitamin D from our sun, daily get your dose of *Son*shine.

Long ago, the sun was used for directions. Today, we have GPS. You simply type in an address, and a voice tells you every turn to make, how many miles the trip will be, and your time of arrival. My granddaughter Devon asked, "Back in your day, Grammie, you didn't have GPS?"

"No, I did not have GPS back in the day. We used maps instead," I explained. I could tell she could not even imagine it. This is like how I have a hard time understanding how, throughout history, explorers used the sun and stars. Today, I cannot imagine how to get direction for my life without following Jesus, can you?

"And we all with unveiled faces contemplate the Lord's glory, are being transformed into his image with ever-increasing glory, which comes from the Lord, who is the Spirit" (2 Corinthians 3:18, NIV). "Be joyful in hope, patient in affliction, faithful in prayer" (Romans 12:12, NIV). Even on rainy days, the "Son" is still shining!

DARK SEASONS

We all know people who have walked through dark

seasons and come out with the greatest reflection of Christ. You may be one of them. "Blessed are you when people hate you, when they exclude you and insult you and reject your name as evil because of the Son of Man. Rejoice in that day and leap for joy because great is your reward in heaven. For that is how their ancestors treated the prophets" (Luke 6:22–23, NIV).

Yes, God's love is poured out through us, but the reality of the Christian faith may not make you popular. Not everyone will like you, and you may not experience a life that is all sunshine and rainbows. God does not promise us a life without dark clouds. However, as a reflection of Him, we know the One who gives light through the darkness. Allow His peace and joy to shine through you. We can do all things when we fully surrender to His plan.

A dear friend of mine suffers from seasonal affective disorder, known as SAD. Her friends know if it is cloudy for days in a row, we need to reach out to her. She will retreat to her home, unable to talk on the phone, and has a difficult time functioning. But when the sun comes out, she forces herself outside to get some sunshine. She is a bright light and the life of the party, so I can't imagine how this lack of sunshine has such a significant effect on her.

In the Bible, there were a few folks who hid from God, or they tried to, such as Adam and Eve, the first couple. "Then the man and his wife heard the sound of the Lord God as He was walking in the garden in the cool of the day, and they hid from the Lord God among the trees" (Genesis 3:8, NKJV). Jonah tried to hide, too. "But Jonah ran away from the Lord and headed for Tarshish" (Jonah 1:3, NIV). Do you ever feel like hiding, running from the talent you know He is calling you to, the dream He wants to fulfill? Is it hard to pull yourself up and face the sunshine? Expose your gift to the light as my friend does. She understands the value of the sun and what it provides in her life.

SIXTY FOR THE DAY

"How priceless is your unfailing love, O God! People take refuge in the shadow of your wings. They feast on the abundance of your house; you give them drink from your river of delights. For with you is the fountain of life; in your light we see light" (Psalm 36:7–9, NIV).

I wish I could make all women sixty just for a day. Just in the same way, I want all young moms to be grandmas for the day. It would change your perspective, but mostly, it would change your self-worth. Something happens with aging, and while it is not a gift to the body, it is a gift to the mind and soul. Aging allows you to understand life is a beautiful gift, and each day is just lovely. I see life through much sunnier lenses these days. The sunny days must be valued and not wasted. You find you are okay with the extra pounds, and the lines have value.

"The Lord is my light and my salvation; whom shall I fear? The Lord is the strength of my life; of whom shall I be afraid?" (Psalm 27:1, NIV). We all have been given a challenge, and some challenges are more obvious, such as a disability, addiction, depression, and lack. However, many challenges are unseen, like abuse, hurt, and great disappointments. But these are all just labels that cannot define who we are. Clear the weeds so the sun can fully shine, and then shine love and kindness to others and yourself. Don't be afraid.

If we allow our shine to be counterfeit, about money, fame, or success, we block the truth; we block the sunshine, love, and kindness. We never know the impact our light has on others. I received a phone call from a friend of many years. She expressed how a choice my husband and I made over thirty years ago made a great impression on her heart and helped her to stand up against something in her own life, clearing some weeds she needed to clear so the sun could fully shine. I didn't know at the time that anyone noticed our stand. I just knew it was not popular as we made that sacrifice. But she saw the effect it had on our family over time. We were blessed as a result of pulling weeds and distancing ourselves from negativity. Shine for others. Be as bright as your creative mind and heart will allow. You are a sunflower!

LET'S DIG IN THE SOIL

You may be a new follower of Christ, or maybe you have been on this road for a while. List the three top struggles you are facing today—no matter how great, no matter how small. Now pray. Just like you need a least fifteen minutes in the sunshine for its health benefits, when you spend even fifteen minutes in prayer or reading a devotional, your spirit greatly benefits and is strengthened. Your soul needs time in the light of the "Son."

Seek your heavenly Father's wisdom and give your burdens to Jesus Christ. You will be amazed. Like a flint, you can set your heart aflame to His plan, bringing true light to the world around you. You can confidently face each day when you spend time facing the "Son." Do not be like Adam and Eve, hiding out in the trees, or running away from the call on your life, like Jonah. Recognize when the Son, Jesus, pulls on your heart to be with Him and run to His glory.

CHAPTER NINE:
SUNFLOWER SEEDS

When we lived in Freeport, Texas, I walked to and from elementary school. Our sweet next-door neighbor Miss. Harris was a widow who had a green thumb, and her garden had the most amazing array of flowers mixed with vegetable and fruit trees. My mom spent hours with her, learning her gardening tips, like *how she grew those large tomato plants and how her hydrangeas were so blue.* Eggshells were her secret; she placed them at the roots of her hydrangeas.

Most mornings, as I cut through her extensive garden, she would pause, garden tools in hand, and looking up from under her oversized hat, she would say, "Hello, Debbie, have a good day." After school, I walked across her backyard on my way home, admiring the smells and colors. But I had a bad habit of picking things, a little rose here and a petal to smell there. Mama caught me a few times and warned me not to touch anything in Miss Harris's garden. However, one day, her shiny, bright red peppers bush caught my eye.

They were tiny little peppers, all pretty and red. I just had to pick one—so I did! As I pulled, it came apart. I dipped my tongue into the pepper seeds, and they burned like a hot fire. Tears filled my eyes, and I quickly rubbed them with pepper juice still on my hands. Well, my sight left me, and I screamed for Mama.

My mom always watched for me out the kitchen window that faced Miss Harris's garden. Hearing her little girl's screams, she came running to my rescue. Through my pain, I learned a big lesson, and oh, did I suffer. The tiny seeds in those small red peppers were hot and powerful. I never picked from Miss Harris's garden again, and Momma banned me from cutting through her garden. I never forgot the power of that small seed.

Gardens are best for flowers and vegetables, but sunflowers love to grow wild in fields, letting their many seeds fall to the ground at the right time while, like waves of golden delight, they shine across open acreage. A sunflower head is composed of 1,000–2,000 tiny flowers joined at the base, and they produce as many seeds as possible. The harvest never looks like the seeds, but in that small pod is the ability to produce many more sunflowers. Once the sunflower sets its face to the east, the seed comes forth and grows into another large sunflower. The sunflower must reach maturity and then sow seeds, not before. Crowned as the top health food in the world, the sunflower seed has a tender texture and nutty taste when roasted. The tasty gray seed is encased in a tear-shaped black-and-white-striped shell. The seeds can be grounded and baked into all kinds of goodies. Also, sunflower oil is a great source of cooking.

Once the seed is planted into the ground, it can begin the growth and maturing process, which is necessary for us as well. As believers, God plants His seed of life inside of us at salvation. When the soil of our hearts is filled with faith, then the seed is sown into good and nourishing soil where it will grow and flourish, but this process takes time. After the seed has matured and grown, the final stage is the harvest. "The harvest is plentiful, but the laborers are few..." (Luke 10:2, NIV). As believers who are a part of God's kingdom, we must also mature and grow in our walk with the Lord before we are ready to reproduce.

TENDING THE SEED

Once planted, a seed needs tending. Tending means you regularly or frequently give something treatment, care, and value. When I think of tending, my husband, Terry, comes to mind. He loves routine, and he is so good about the little things in life, like locking up, turning off lights, making the bed, and keeping the pantry stocked. The car is always washed, and the oil is changed. He was very dedicated to our garden, and he worked hours to weed, feed, and plant the seasonal plants. But he always started with a good seed.

The mustard seed in the Bible is our example of the kingdom of heaven. "And He said to them, 'Because of the littleness of your faith; for truly I say to you, if you have faith of a mustard seed, you will say to this mountain, 'Move from here to there,' and it will move, and nothing will be impossible for you'" (Matthew 17:20, NIV). "The apostles said to the Lord, 'Increase our faith like a mustard seed!' He replied, 'If you have faith as small as a mustard seed, you would say to the mulberry tree, 'Be uprooted and be planted in the sea,' and it would obey you'" (Luke 17:5–6, NIV). The tiny mustard seed grows a large bunch of mustard. The mustard seed is not concerned with size— it is going to grow! When you pray and ask for mountains to be moved, financial, health, and a child in trouble, don't concern yourself with the size of your prayers. In planting seeds, size does not matter—faith does. So tend to your seeds of faith through prayer.

We all desire healing and wholeness for our hearts and minds, but for this to happen, we must tend the garden of our souls and spirits through God's grace. Bringing our broken pieces to Jesus is necessary for our personal tending and growth. However, sometimes our spiritual growth can feel more like a child who fell and scraped their knee. As an adult, I learned how not to skin my knees by slowing down. In the same way, we can't be in a hurry to grow spiritually because it takes time, but the results are worth the process. Seeds of greatness, joy, peace, and love come from maturity; the gifts of the maturing process are seeds of creativity, goodness, love, and kindness that are full and ripe in our minds and hearts. But how do we know we have grown when there is no magic age?

Wait on God's timing; then, strength will come. Many of us force growth by trying to produce something that is out of season. But some seeds may not be ripe; they may not be ready for harvesting. And the seed that falls to the ground too soon will not take root. "But they who wait for the Lord shall renew their strength; they shall mount up with wings like eagles; they shall run and not be weary; they shall walk and not faint" (Isaiah 40:31, KJV). It takes strength to sow a seed, and it takes wisdom to be patient. You will know when you are ready to go for that dream in your heart, but for now, patiently sow seeds of greatness.

Words are seeds we plant each day in the hearts of those around us. Daily, through care and effort, we are to plant loving words (seeds) into the hearts of our children and loved ones. Plant words of respect and admiration in your husband and words of honor in your parents. It can be so easy with our friends to plant life-giving words, "Oh, Susan, you are so sweet, kind, and talented. What cute shoes, have you lost a few pounds?" But sometimes, we can become lax in planting seeds of kindness in those closest to us, like children, spouses, adult siblings, or aging parents. Be alert in these areas to plant good seeds so you will have life-giving fruit when the harvest comes.

However, the hardest seeds to sow are the seeds we plant in our minds called *heart talk*. There is a serious syndrome known as impostor syndrome. This syndrome is the internal mental experience of feeling like a fake in some area of one's life. This syndrome also causes people to doubt their talents or skills in a particular area, causing the affected person to struggle with self-doubt or dread of being exposed for who they think they really are. This relates to those of us who tell ourselves we don't deserve the gifts and talents

God blessed us with. How can I possibly be a sunflower? I told myself I could not write a book. It was too big of a dream. Who would read it or want to? Even a few of my friends laughed at my dream. But then I sowed new seeds: I can do all things in Christ; I am fearfully and wonderfully made. "If you abide in me, and my words [seeds] abide in you, ask whatever you wish, and it will be done for you" (John 15:7, ESV).

WAIT ON HIM

Where does your seed come from? Who planted you in this kingdom garden? In the story of Abraham, we find our connection. "If you belong to Christ, then you are Abraham's seed and heirs according to the promise" (Galatians 3:29, NIV). "I will make you into a great nation, and I will bless you; I will make your name great, and you will be a blessing" (Genesis 12:2, NIV). The seed in our hearts comes from the promise and blessing of our father of faith, Abraham. He was called to leave his family, travel to an unknown place, and settle in a land far away, trusting that God's plan for him was perfect. He had great faith, but God had to change his identity and his name, along with his wife's, Sarah. Then he had to wait for the promise, but Sarah was impatient, trying to create the promise before the season.

Like Sarah, our stress and anxiety come when we force God's plan and try to harvest out of season. We know His promises like Sarah and Rebekah knew God had a planned promise, but these great women came up with their own plan B. They could not wait! Ladies, some of us are very good at charm and getting what we want when we want it, but the fruit of control is stress and dysfunction. I watch many young women struggle with so much stress because they are trying to accomplish a blessing on their own, and they harvest out of season.

Young women with a promised calling must experience the process of maturing through waiting. The farmer works hard to get the harvest out on time, but then he waits. Like the sunflower seeds will pop out at the perfect time, God will establish your promised purpose at the right time, so wait on Him. Do not push your calendar and body to the very limit—taking classes and studying late hours. Pushing yourself will only rob you of needed growth for the harvest time.

Attune to how much strength and grace you have and what season God has you in. Maybe you are in the season of small children, working a job, or both. We are so unique, and our callings and giftings are vast. Do not let go of your dreams just because you are in a season when you can't pursue them. Instead, use this time to develop intimacy with God through prayer. Ask God to give you wisdom during the waiting period of growth. In due season, the dream will come to pass. When the season for harvest comes, you can freely move into that place of production. It will come quickly.

DRESSED FOR PLANTING

The farmer puts her overalls on and heads out to the field, ready to pick, plow, mow, and do whatever needs to be done. She plans for the work she is called to. She watches the weather and the seasons because she must sow the right seed at the right time. If she doesn't plant in the right season, then she will miss the harvest completely. There is harvest all around us, but sometimes we miss our seed planting because of distractions that were not even in the field.

Do you recall *Green Acres*, a TV show from the '60s? A New York lawyer and his wife, played by Eva Gabor, move into an old run-down farm. The husband, Oliver Wendell Douglas, played by Eddie Albert, wants a quiet life. At the start of each show, Oliver would drive the tractor wearing a suit and tie. Lisa, his socialite wife, would be in an evening gown. The contrast is comical because they are not dressed for the season or situation they are in.

We need to dress for the part and season every day. If we embark on our day not dressed for our season or situation, we will miss the opportunity to sow seeds into the lives of others. You may see someone you know, and you should say, "Hello. How are you?" throwing some seeds of kindness their way, but you don't because you weren't dressed for the season or situation. You were caught off guard. Many times, I have felt the pull to bless someone but was not in my harvest attire. I did not plan to work the field that day and was caught out of my spiritual overalls. There were times I knew God was pulling me to encourage someone, but sadly, I missed the season, and I missed the harvest. Now, I start each day dressing with intention. I choose to look my best so that I can confidently be a blessing and sow kindness in whichever field God sends me. In the same way, put on the full armor of God each day, and don't leave your house without putting on your spiritual overalls.

MY LITTLE LAMB

On the farm, I learned a lesson about little lambs the hard way. We had just moved from Texas, and I discovered a little lamb down in the barn. I named him Taffy right away, and climbing in the pin, Taffy and I started to play. This story will not end like my Amy the goat story did in *I Made the Rainbow,* so read on. Playing around, I pulled at Taffy's tail; to my horror, it came off in my little hand. I started to scream, and my poor mama came running; she did a lot of that, trying to raise me! It was hard to console a nine-year-old who thought she had dismembered a little baby lamb. I learned that my timing was just right and that a ring had been placed on Taffy's tail so that it would fall off naturally. I was a little ahead of the moment, and I had helped it along, but Taffy was going to be okay. He was not crying, only me.

SEEDS OF VALUE

In the seventeenth century, because they valued their seed, Holland tulip prices were said to be as high as the price of a house. The market sets the value of the seed based on how rare the seed is and public demand. Today, saffron is selling for 5,000–10,000 dollars a pound. In the world of art, the value of a piece is based on who the artist is. We have all seen an art piece where the canvas looks like a child could have painted it, yet we are shocked by its high price. We watch as it sells for greater value than a home because of who the artist was. As God's masterpiece, your value has nothing to do with the markets, your popularity, or how rare you are—although you are one of a kind—it's based on Who made you and Who He says you are. "For You formed my inmost being; You knit me together in my mother's womb. I praise You, for I am fearfully and wonderfully made. Marvelous are Your works, and I know this very well" Psalm 139:13–14, BSB).

You are a seed of great value. You are so valuable that God sent His one and only Son, Jesus Christ, to die on the cross for you so you could spend eternity with your Maker in heaven. Romans 10:9 (BSB) tells us, "If you confess with your mouth, 'Jesus is Lord,' and believe in your heart that God raised Him from the dead, you will be saved." If you haven't already done this, take a moment now to acknowledge Jesus as your Lord and Savior. Ask Him to forgive you of your sins and confess aloud that He is Lord of your life. Next, tell someone and plant yourself in a Bible-believing church.

THE SOWER

Sow seeds of love with actions,

Sow seeds of beauty with care,

Sow seeds of joy with laughter,

But you must stay aware.

The field is all around you.

Your heart, so full of pride,

As you look upon the harvest the Master did provide.

Sowing seeds of kindness to all within your reach.

Seeing growth aplenty most perfect and complete.

Keep sowing, sister.

Sow with words you speak each day,

And reap the peace of Jesus as you journey on your way.

HARVEST

Sow seeds at the right time, but plant the right seeds because what we plant, we will harvest. We can plant seeds of discord and discouragement, or we can plant seeds of greatness, love, and humility. What will you plant? Our minds are like fields we daily plant seeds into. And our self-talk also plants seeds. If we plant corn, we will not grow wheat. A poppy seed will not produce a rose. If you plant negative thoughts and meditate on them, it will produce negative character and choices.

The best seeds are seeds of hope, love, and goodness sown daily in our garden of life. Watch those seeds spring to life in due season. What harvest has God promised you? What seeds are you planting to receive His promised harvest? How is the waiting as you watch the garden? Just keep planting those seeds, and trust His timing for His harvest in your life.

Farming is one of the hardest jobs, and we have fewer farmers today than ever before. Small family farms that have been passed down for generations are falling by the wayside. The only way to see the harvest is to labor and sow seeds, but the laborers are fewer. In the same way, the kingdom of God has a harvest and a small labor force. When we plant seeds, we labor in the field, but later, we will watch the seeds take root and produce a harvest. I have watched a young woman labor in her marriage, planting love and hope. In faith, she toiled over her marriage garden. Then one day, she called me with her praise report of what God had done in her marriage. We rejoiced with shouts of joy at the harvest. Her words, "You won't believe this, but we could talk about this issue, and we didn't get upset." She sowed seeds of honor and service, and then she enjoyed the fruit of her labor.

I prayed with another friend about her teenager, and together, we planted seeds of faith. This mother worked in her field, and she never gave up, even during the darkest times of addiction. She sowed. She planted seeds of tough love, and then she waited for the harvest. Suddenly, she looked up and saw the fruit of her labor. Her son was set free from drugs and walking in freedom. She and I had a harvest party. Her son is still free today, but now he is planting his own seeds of faith in his garden. "Then He said to his disciples. 'The harvest is plentiful, but the laborers are few. Therefore, pray earnestly to the lord of the harvest to send out laborers into his harvest'" (Matthew 9:37–38, ESV). Remember, roots grow unseen, so like the farmer waiting for the harvest, be patient.

The seeds we plant must be seeds for harvest. And you can throw out any bad batches of seeds by changing the conversation in your mind. Like the farmer planning to plant corn, plan to plant positive words. You might ask, "But how about when I feel unvalued or unloved?" See your mind like a nest, with thoughts flying in and out like little birds. When the negative thought hits your nest, shoo it away quickly. Then invite another bird into the nest. Say, "I am valued; I am loved; I am wanted; I am God's special treasure; I am His queen; I am dearly loved by my heavenly Father." Let that positive seed take root, and watch and see the harvest. The bird in the nest analogy is a great way to help children understand their thought lives. Children are visual, and you can ask them, "What little birds have been in your nest today?" When you think, *I can't*, remind yourself of what you have done. Remind yourself of your accomplishments and victories. But most importantly, remember the goodness of the Lord and all the ways He has rescued and delivered you in the past. Bring to remembrance His great works, and set your mind on things above, not on things below. This is a fresh seed for the soul.

SOWING KINDNESS

Brethren, I do not count myself to have apprehended: but one thing I do, forgetting those things which are behind and reaching forward to those things which are ahead, I press toward the goal for the prize of the upward call of God in Christ Jesus. Therefore let us, as many as are mature, have this mind, and if in anything you think otherwise, God will reveal even this to you.

Philippians 3:13–15 (NKJV)

Lack of planning is a big "sow" stopper. But using time wisely and using a calendar are important harvest tools. So many things pull on our time, and we can get caught up in a million things that suck it away. Manage your harvest. Ask yourself this question, "What have I said 'no' to that I really wanted to say 'yes' to? What is on my plate that is not seed-bearing?" Let the show (sow) begin! "And God said, 'See, I have given you every herb that yields seed which is on the face of the earth and every tree whose fruit yields seed; to you, it shall be for food'" (Genesis 1:29, NKJV).

At my dinner table, I wanted my babies to talk about their day, so I came up with a way to encourage conversation through a game called "thumbs up and thumbs down." Then I would ask, "What was the best part of your day, and what was the worst?" It made for pleasant table talk, with each child taking a turn in the conversation, but the focus was all on them. As they hit their teen years, I changed my question to "What acts of kindness did you do today? What seeds did they sow?" This was challenging because they did not know what they could do at school for others. I remember my granddaughter (eleven at the time) saying, "I turned in my homework, Grammie!" I gave them ideas, like buying a cookie for the less popular kid, telling someone they looked nice that day, holding a door open, or bringing the teacher a flower just because and telling her, "Thank you for teaching me." What a fun harvest this has been. I now ask them to text me when they sow an act of kindness.

LET'S DIG IN THE SOIL

God asks us to sow seeds of time and finance. Many times, our seeds will be a sacrifice. His timing may be inconvenient for us. But He will always give you the grace to sow. If the fruit of your life is not sweet, check what you're planting. "He who observes the wind will not sow, And he who regards the clouds will not reap" (Ecclesiastes 11:4, NKJV).

What seeds have you sown today? The farmer can't wait for the perfect day to plant seeds. You cannot wait until your life is all worked out to sow the seed God has trusted you with. Plant seeds of faith, kindness, love, understanding, and courage today. Throw away any bad seeds of doubt, discord, anger, and hate. Think about the words spoken by you and to you just today. Do they need to be tossed out or left to take root in your heart?

A HARVEST RECIPE

To harvest love, sow action
To harvest joy, sow laughter
To harvest beauty, sow care
To harvest kindness, sow peace
To harvest happiness, sow good times.

Take some time right now and think about the past twenty-four hours. Based on today, what harvest can you expect to receive? Did you let the cloudy day or stormy wind stop you? What and where did you sow today? Did you sow seeds in your marriage, your children, a dear friend, or even in your heart and mind? Maybe a group you meet with? Take heart, farmer girl. The crop is coming!

CHAPTER TEN:
SUNFLOWERS AND BEES

One spring day, still in my Sunday best, I was out playing chase with my younger brothers. Laughing, we ran across fields tagging each other and yelling, "You're it!" Stretched across our farm was a creek where a large tree had fallen, making a bridge to the other side. Somehow, my brothers got on either side of the creek. Trapped, I headed across the log while my brothers yelled, "We got you now!" when, suddenly, I heard a buzzing sound and felt a sting. Hidden in the old log was a beehive. Having disturbed their nest by running across the fallen tree, the bees flew right up my dress, stinging my belly. Screaming, I ran as fast as I could while smashing the bees through my dress, which made the painful stings worse by the second. Wailing in pain, I looked for my mamma—again.

I love bees and have a few pieces of jewelry that feature them. The western honeybee is the best-known bee species. I took a photo of a carpenter bee with its black and shiny gold body. My name, Deborah, means queen bee. And who does not like honey? The bee makes a significant contribution to the world. It is said that every third spoonful we eat depends on the pollination of the bees, which we celebrate on May 20 each year for World Bee Day. And a land flowing with milk and honey was promised to Israel in Deuteronomy 6:3. I imagine there must have been some large beehives in the Promised Land.

Pollination is anything that carries pollen from the male part of the plant to the female part. Bees and pollination are so important to the development of the sunflower's seeds, but the bee is not attracted to a lone sunflower. Bees are attracted to a field full of many flowers. In the same way that sunflowers need each other for pollination, we need one another too. Strong relationships attract the bees, but mostly, they give us pollination.

Some plants are self-pollinating, while others depend on the wind and insects. In the same way, we grow through relationships and learning from others. From 2020 through 2021, we experienced a season many had not seen before. With COVID-19 lockdowns, many found themselves isolated—no one to stir up, no personal touch. The effects of this season may show in our society for many years to come, proving the deep need we have for one another. To "bee" hugged, loved, and cared for. Like sunflowers, we grow through pollination.

Today, many issues arise from loneliness and isolation. While our society connects through social media, we lack genuine connections. The family connection is more important than ever, and while the dinner table is valued, it is used less and less. Needs go untended: the child is being bullied, the girl doesn't feel popular, the single mother is raising her children without help, the adult is caring for an ill parent—many suffer in silent isolation. The wounded and hurt person thinks, *No one cares about me.* We must tend to the desires of our hearts and the hearts of those we are in a relationship with through time, attention, and care.

What do you want to be? Personally, I want to change; I want to grow; I want to be successful, and I want to be loved. Growing up, I had lots of *want to "bees."* I wanted to be married; I wanted to be a mom; I wanted to be an interior designer. I wanted to do these things with all my heart. I hoped and prayed my "bees" would all come true.

One day, I no longer wanted to be: I was a wife, I had a baby, and I worked at my interior design company. But being and becoming are two different things. I had the titles of "mom," "wife," and "businesswoman," but I lacked the skill. The truth of *becoming* is different from the truth of being. So, my *bes* changed to *I want to be a good wife and be a better mom.* I desired to become a talented designer, but I needed to gather knowledge from other skilled people. My growth would have ended if I knew it all. God brought many people into my life, and many came because of my prayers. I prayed for God to send help, and He always did.

The trust and faith we have in others pollinate our souls. The belief then becomes the treasure that makes dreams come true. "So then faith comes by hearing and hearing by the word of God" (Romans 10:17, NKJV). Seeds of faith and the Word of God are priceless. "Therefore, I say to you, whatever things you ask for when you pray, believe that you receive them, and you will have them" (Mark 11:24, NKJV). Unbelief is our enemy and the destroyer of our dreams. Believe God can do great things in and through you, and extend that belief to others so they can be all they are called to be as well.

THE BEEHIVE

The beehive is fascinating; all the bees know they have a job to do. The hive runs perfectly; everything centers around the queen. During her most productive season, she will lay over two to three thousand eggs per day. Worker bees make up 90 percent of the hive. Mostly female, they live about thirty days and go to work the moment they hatch. Communication among the bees comes in the form of dance. They express information about the distance and direction of nectar in the waggle dance. The dance language is one of the great wonders of science. A church is like a beehive, and having a church family is essential for growth. Your beehive or church is a place where others support you, stir up your gifts, and pollinate you with faith. Church is a place where bee lovers come together. Believe you have seeds of greatness planted in you. Believe in change, and trust God to bring it.

According to some naturalists, without the bee, humanity would die in four years because of the huge part bees play in our ecosystem as one of our key pollinators. Smell or color attracts bees to the flower, and the pollen sticks to the bee's body. The bee does not pick it up, and it is unaware of the important job it is doing. The little bee does not know the world's food supply depends on it. It is a bee allowing the pollen to stick and then fall off on the next flower. And so, the sowing of pollen goes.

The bee is not thinking about the pollen as it gets the nectar's sweetness from the flower. The pollination just happens. As we receive the sweet Spirit from our heavenly Father, we gather wisdom, then one day, words of encouragement come from our lips to a friend because what we plant inside us will flow out of us sooner or later, and like pollen, we can feed and nourish the souls of those we are in a relationship with. You might be unaware of your value, but as you fill up with the pollen of God's Word, it will overflow from you into the hearts of others. Through your words, be kind to yourself and be kind to others. "Gracious speech is like clover honey—good taste to the soul, quick energy" (Proverbs 16:24, MSG).

The sunflowers' bright golden color attracts the bee. In the same way, as believers, we pick up faith, love, and hope from one another—it just sticks. As we become filled with the Holy Spirit, we cannot help but become more attractive to others as we make deposits in those around us. Have you noticed how people are drawn to you? Have you been outside wearing a favorite perfume and had a bee buzz you? I know Christian women who wear the perfume of grace. I am attracted to these sweet sisters. Like the bright color of the sunflower, they pull me in.

BUSY BEE

Bees sleep five to eight hours at night, and some roll over on their side. It's hard to tell when the bee is asleep because its eyes do not close. Are you a busy bee—never sitting down, always doing, hard to rest and relax? Do you feel there are never enough hours in the day for your long lists of to-dos? I know women who struggle with guilt when they enjoy a break because they get their value based on how much they accomplish each day.

Lists make you intentional about your day, but when using a list, make sure to keep your focus on whatever *petal* you are in. Lists also help us set boundaries for ourselves because they reveal areas we may need to adjust as *busy bees*. I'm a list maker and encourage others to do so, but I have a way of planning my day I would like to share. At the top, I write, "To be successful today." Then I limit my list to only seven to-dos for the day. I make an appointment for devotional time right at the top. This can be as soon as my eyes open. Due to my work, I list timed appointments, but many items are flexible. I try to only book two face-to-face meetings a day. And I plan time for emails and phone calls, so that is always one of the seven. But make sure that each week, you prioritize time for connecting with friends and family and for self-care. This ensures you have time for joy.

On my list is a connection with a friend, be it a quick phone call, coffee, or lunch date. Then I have something on the list just for me, which could be a couple of hours of reading a book I enjoy, getting my nails done, having my hair styled, or getting a facial. I love painting, cooking, and connecting with those I love, so I make room for this every week on my list. Self-care might be as simple as a thirty-minute bubble bath. For me, planning to paint or get to bed early is a treat. I have an art studio, and painting each day brings me so much joy. Identify what brings you joy, and make time for it in your day.

Sunday, no list is required because that is my day of rest. At day's end, I may not have all seven to-dos completed, but I accomplished something with my time. In the early years of my design business, working through lunch and never breaking for even a cup of coffee described many of my days. I was running on empty, but one day, I decided, as my own boss, I would order myself to have work hours. I try for four to six hours each day.

I love interior design work, and it takes time to have good design, but I also love being Grammie, having time to make dinner for Terry, having time for ministry, and writing. These are things I value. I do not want my grandchildren to say, "Grammie never sat down and enjoyed the Christmas dinner; she did not have time for our family." In the past, I watched my sweet mother-in-law sitting exhausted in the living room chair while she told us to eat without her, having baked for two weeks before the Christmas meal.

Rearrange your life plan so you can have breaks. When you run on empty, you will have nothing to give. Do not be a busy bee. I have pushed the gas tank in the past and lived on fumes, but I'm no fun to be around, nor do I like myself when I'm out of gas. Dave Ramsey is a "tell it like it is" financial teacher. He is upfront when he says if you do not live on a budget, you will go broke. Similarly, if you do not live by a plan or plan your time, you will be bankrupted emotionally, wondering why you have no joy or sweetness in life. Ask yourself, "To 'bee' successful today, what do I need to do?"

QUEEN BEE DEBORAH

Now Deborah, a prophetess, the wife of Lapidoth, was judging Israel. And she would sit under the palm tree of Deborah between Ramah and Bethel in the mountains of Ephraim, and the children of Israel came up to her for judgment. Then, she sent and called for Barak the son of Abinoam from Kedesh in Naphtali, and said to him, "Has not the Lord God of Israel commanded, 'Go and deploy troops at mount tabor; take with you ten thousand men of the sons of Naphtali and of the sons of Zebulun: and against you I will deploy Sisera the commander of Jabin's army, with his chariots and his multitude at the river Kisbon: and I will deliver him into your hand?'" ... So, she said, "I will surely go with you; nevertheless, there will be no glory for you in the journey you are taking, for the Lord will sell Sisera into the hand of a woman." Then Deborah arose and went with Barak to Kedesh. And Barak called

Zebulun and Naphtali to Kedesh; he went with ten thousand men under his command, and Deborah went up with him.

Judges 4:4–10 (NKJV)

Deborah was one of the great women in the Bible. This story is so fascinating in that she had her own palm tree for an outdoor office. Not only did she judge Israel, but she told Barak what to do and how to do it. And then, guess what? He listened! But Barak didn't get any credit for the victory. The story goes on, and Sisera falls into the hands of a woman—Jael.

And Jael went out to meet Sisera and said to him, "Turn aside with me; do not fear." And when he turned aside with her into the tent, she covered him with a blanket. Then he said to her, "Please, give me a little water to drink, for I am thirsty." So, she opened a jug of milk, gave him a drink, and covered him ... Then, Jael, Heber's wife, took a tent peg and took a hammer in her hand, and went softly to him and drove the peg into his temple, and it went into the ground: he died.

Judges 4:18–21 (NKJV)

Think about the spirit of hospitality this woman clearly had and the bravery she had to ask him in and give him milk and a blanket. She was wise. These brave women surely were mothers. Deborah had a career, a place of leadership and honor. Women back in that day were not looked to for leadership roles, but no one told her she could not fly. I wonder how many women pollinated Deborah's life. Had her mom or grandmother told her she was strong or that she would be a great leader and she could stand tall and be heard?

Jael, I want to meet her one day. I imagine she was not powerful looking. She must have had a sweet and kind spirit for Sisera to trust her. All of us are on a journey, and we have experienced difficult times and perhaps made hard choices. God uses women in mighty ways, no matter what they have experienced. I pray women would rise in the kingdom and set their hearts to do the King's bidding. Don't give up, no matter what you are experiencing right now.

BLESSED AND WOUNDED

Harvest comes from being a part of something and working within a group. Sadly, many hurts have resulted from the stings of church groups. We all have been wounded Christians. If you have ever done anything for the kingdom, you have experienced some form of a sting in this area. Church hurts happen to everyone because we attend church with real people, not saints. I went to church for many years with the idea, *What can the church do for me? What am I receiving?* I attended church services, sitting back with the attitude, *I'm here. I'm ready to receive.* But one day, I realized the church was not about me; it was about the kingdom and His plan.

One year, the church I attended hosted a missionary fair.

We transformed the rooms into countries, and there was a food counter with food from each region. We had a family fun evening planned. Missionaries would be our honored guests, and this would be a great event. They assigned me to India. I had elephants cut out of wood, and I painted them with layers of glue and gray paint to look and feel like elephant skin. I displayed a tiger as one entered the room through a walkway lined with reeds and grass, which led to a vibrant marketplace with beautiful silks and pottery. I created a photo booth with Indian attire, Indian rugs, and a painting on a large canvas of Jesus reaching down to the children of India. The aromas of India's spices filled the air from my slow cooker, and I had girls serving delicacies while wearing traditional Indian saris. The saris were an array of bright, beautiful colors, and I wore one too.

The missionary from India was so moved he shed a tear or two as our pastor and his wife went on and on. I could not have been prouder or worked harder. The silk tapestry wall hanging spelled out the words "Pray for India." I had worked for days and days. However, the night before, there had been an appreciation dinner for all the volunteers to thank us and celebrate our hard work. We had invested so much time and worked late into many nights, and the rooms were amazing.

The man overseeing this event stood up and thanked us for our labor of love. Then he said, "This is not a design competition. It is not about how great your room looks!" My mind went blank. I had worked so hard and given my all. I felt like his words were directed at me. I was the only designer in the room. I was afraid that he felt like I was showing everyone up. *How could he think that I would want to show off? I just wanted to do my best; I wanted the church to shine. He could have just come to me, not called me out in front of everyone; the whole room knows he is talking about me.* I worked the next evening's event downcast, and my heart wasn't in it. *Who cares?* I thought. I just need to quit this church. *They are not Christians*, my immature spirit and mind thought. I could not sleep. All my thoughts kept replaying his words. I had worked so hard, but I felt undermined by this man.

Finally, I realized when we have hurt or a wound, we are to go and talk to them. So I did. To my surprise, this man did not know I was in the design business, nor was he referring to me at all. He thought my room was fabulous, and he was grateful. He had just made a statement, thinking it would make everyone feel good about the work they had invested. Many people do not shine in the glory God gives them. Many hide gifts in fear of rejection or because of the foolish words of another or hurts and misunderstandings, as I experienced during the missionary fair. Now, I always assume the best about what others say and do.

BEE STINGS

My nickname for my Terry is "Honey Bun." When we were dating, he sent letters, and he drew little bees on his cards and notes. But what stops the pollen flow is the sting. We do not enjoy honey because of the sting. Beekeepers purposely get stung about ten times to build a tolerance to bee venom. Then, future stings hurt and swell less as the beekeepers tend the hive and harvest the honey. The sweetness in our lives many times comes with a few stings.

The hurt of the missionary event would not be a big deal today. I've grown as a Christian, and with that growth comes understanding, patience, and perspective. I've had a few stings, and now I know they are no big deal if I want the honey. I watched a beekeeper reach in with bare hands and remove hives. She had so much experience she could tell if a hive had sweet bees or if she needed to wear her guard. Just by the sound of the buzzing, she knew if they would sting her.

What an ear to hear she has. To be a fully mature sunflower, we must keep reaching for the sweetness in life, the honey, and not worry about a few stings on the way. Know when to guard your heart and wear the armor of faith.

"You're just a bee charmer, Idgie Threadgoode. That's what you are, a bee charmer."

—Fannie Flagg in the movie *Fried Green Tomatoes*[10]

So, how do we charm bees? With sweetness—honey, like sweet words, should flow. One day, my friend's daughter flooded their home because she accidentally left the sink in the upstairs bathroom running all night long. They awoke to major damage and costly repairs. But her wise mom covered her with sweet love and wisdom. She knew how bad she felt. This same daughter had lovingly cared for, supported, and cooked for her mom through cancer, prayed with her, and fasted. She also knew that this was truly a mistake due to her long study hours.

My friend loved her daughter and forgave her instantly, covering the difficulty with sweet honey.

I thought about my girls—could I have been so gracious? Sad to say, but I do not think I would have responded with such sweetness and kindness. Now I could since others have pollinated my life with their goodness and kindness. I watched as women showed me faith beyond measure. Like the bee, I should not be able to fly. I did not have the education or the perfect home life. The facts are my parents were both dropouts and teenagers when I was born. But seeds of faith took hold of me, and I sowed the seed of belief in my mind that the favor of God was upon me. Then I could fly. You have the King's favor; you have seeds that will lift you higher and higher. Allow the pollen and love from others to pour over you. God wants to call out your gifts. He will teach you how to charm bees and get all the honey and sweetness out of life—no matter the stings.

On the farm, we had a dump, a large area back in the field where all the leftover, broken-down equipment went to be. I loved the dump. It was a great resource for my creative inventions. Many items found their way to my playhouse. My twin brothers were six years old. And my dad had my brother Wayne working with him on the tractor. They had been working around the dump and came across a large beehive. They barely made it out of the area without getting stung.

As we sat down for dinner that evening, my youngest

brother, James, was missing. Dad asked us if we knew where he might be. Wayne spoke up, "I think he may be at the dump." Dad was concerned and sent me to find him. I came across him on the lane crying out in pain. We could not count the stings because there were too many. He became very sick. Interestingly, as an adult, he was stung by a bee, and the doctor told him he had a bee allergy. He had forgotten about being stung as a boy, so I reminded him.

As we are all in the field of life, we must understand that hurts and stings will come our way. But we must have mercy for those with adverse reactions to the hurt, like watching a friend who has been stung, so to speak. Some may never recover from the stings of life because they wear it like a badge, and they cannot allow healing and understanding to heal their heart. However, God can give us all victory over life's stings. Becoming a victor isn't easy. The Word tells us, "O death, where is thy sting? O grave, where is thy victory?" (1 Corinthians 15:55–57, KJV). If we can have victory over death and the grave, then victory can come over past hurts. The Father desires for you to be healed and to be a great sunflower.

GREAT FAITH TO BEE

According to all known laws of aviation, there is no way that a bee can fly. Its wings are too small to get its little fat body off the ground. But bees fly anyway because they are unaware of this fact.[11] They are a little wonder of the universe every time they take flight. The bee does not say,

"I can't fly; my wings are too small," or, "I can't fly; my body is too fat!" No, they just believe they can fly, and they do. We can take a lesson from the bees and have faith that, yes, we can. What are you "*bee*lieving" for? Let it take flight!

Faith means you don't worry because God's Word says, "So why do you worry about clothing? Consider the lilies of the field, how they grow; they neither toil nor spin" (Matthew 6:28, NKJV). God knows our every need, and He will provide for us. We are blessed to be a blessing. In the sermon on the mount, Jesus gave the blessings sermon known as the Beatitudes in the book of Matthew.

> *Blessed are the poor in spirit, for theirs is the kingdom of heaven.*
>
> *Blessed are they that mourn, for they shall be comforted.*
>
> *Blessed are the meek; for they shall inherit the earth.*
>
> *Blessed are those that hunger and thirst for righteousness, for they shall be filled.*
>
> *Blessed are the merciful, for they shall obtain mercy.*
>
> *Blessed are the pure in heart, for they shall see God.*
>
> *Blessed are the peacemakers, for they shall be called sons of God.*

Blessed are those who are persecuted for righteousness' sake, for theirs is the kingdom of heaven.

Matthew 5:3–10 (NKJV)

LET'S DIG

A honeybee pollinates unintentionally, and it stings when it feels threatened. Similarly, as Christians, we get to intentionally pollinate, lift up others, and "bee" ready and on the lookout for daily ways to spread love and hope around us. Choose to be a honeybee and watch your stinger!

Do you have dreams with a sting attached to them? List them now, and take the time to write the dreams that need pollinating. List the sting that stopped the dream. Now ask the Father to remove the stinger and "bee" all you can "bee." Stop believing the lie. Believe you can fly, and you will!

CHAPTER ELEVEN:

RESTING IN THE HARVEST

Like the sunflower, we grow in rest and in light. Rest is vital to your growth, and the only way to be the star you have been called to be is to get proper rest. Valuable sleep and relaxation are key ingredients to learning how to unplug from work and media. In my workaholic season, I struggled to understand rest—the Sabbath. I truly felt I needed it, and it was for my good, but I just couldn't take one. I heard sermons on how we needed to have a day out of seven when we fully rested our bodies and minds, but I never felt right about taking a restful day.

I would try to have a day to lie around, have fun, watch some TV, and not work, or I would take a day and be in nature to pray, fast, and read the Word. But I struggled with *unrest*, and it wasn't in my comfort zone. So, I prayed about it. *Is it me? Why is this day uncomfortable?*

Then the answer came. The day of rest, the Sabbath, is a day about trust. If you cannot trust God to do in six days what you would like to do in seven, you are not trusting God fully.

In his book *Take the Day Off*, Pastor Robert Morris[12] addresses a day of rest from a new perspective by showing how it is listed right there with "Thou shalt not kill, Thou shalt not steal" (Romans 13:9, KJV), the number four commandment. "Remember the Sabbath day, to keep it holy" (Exodus 20:8, NKJV). This commandment comes with the most given instructions, right up there with "Thou shalt not make unto thee any graven image [carved idols]" (Exodus 20:4, KJV). The Sabbath is not about me getting rest. It is about me trusting Him and having a day that is pleasing to Him.

I love what the psalmist David wrote in Psalm 23:1–2 (NLT), "The Lord is my shepherd; I have all that I need. He lets me rest in green meadows; He leads me beside peaceful streams." God wants to lead us in peace, and He wants us to rest. The color green is considered the most relaxing color, and the psalmist describes how God wants us to rest in green meadows. Also, this passage is speaking of pastures comprising tender green grass because God not only wants to deal tenderly with us, but He wants us to deal tenderly with ourselves. God wants His daughters to rest in tender green places, where there is life and health, but for this to happen, we have to agree with Him—we have to *trust*.

The sheep could stubbornly stay standing in the green

pastures, "baaing" at the shepherd that they are "just fine" and arguing that they do not need to lie down. Or the sheep could receive the shepherd's tender care and lay down in the pastures of tenderness. First Corinthians 2:5 (NIV) speaks to this idea of resting in God's wisdom, "So that your faith might not rest on human wisdom, but on God's power." I don't know about you, but I want to rest in God's tenderness, trusting in Him to provide for all my needs.

For some of us, the way we were raised may affect our perspective of rest and whether or not we feel worthy of it. For example, my dad used to say, "Why walk across the street when you can run?" I had to look at my past to see how messages like this may have influenced my view of rest and whether I felt like I could rest or not. For a longtime, I didn't give myself permission to rest because I didn't trust God would take care of all my needs. Thankfully, God has changed this area in my life, and now I prioritize rest each day and take a Sabbath. Not letting yourself lie down in green meadows is a form of worry.

Worry is a set of thoughts that cause us to feel upset or stressed. In Greek, it is a divided mind or someone who is "double-minded." When we want to harvest peace, we have to pay attention to worrisome thoughts and keep our minds renewed because worry kills our harvest, and it kills our joy. Jesus told us we don't need to worry about anything.

> *That is why I tell you not to worry about everyday life—whether you have enough food and drink, or enough clothes to wear. Isn't life more than food, and your body more*

than clothing? Look at the birds. They don't plant or harvest or store food in barns, for your heavenly Father feeds them. And aren't you far more valuable to him than they are? Can all your worries add a single moment to your life?

Matthew 6:25–27 (NLT)

It's pleasing to the Father when we rest or do things that bring us joy. Now, my rest days are full of joy, and I feel refreshed. The best part is that I do more in my six days than I ever did in my seven. My work is more successful. Psalm 46:10a (NIV) states, "Be still, and know that I am God." Psalm 100:3 (NIV) also says, "Know that the LORD is God. It is he who made us, and we are his; we are his people, the sheep of his pasture." God wants to be our Good Shepherd, and He wants us to rest in tender pastures, so trust Him and let yourself rest.

EVEN LAND NEEDS REST

I loved harvest time on our Ohio farm—riding the tractor with Grandpa, the smells of fresh-cut corn, hay, and the busyness of the workers. We had a large tractor and a combine. The tractor did many jobs, but the combine only gathered the harvest. The large machine hit the field, clearing the harvest, gliding up the rows, and cutting the corn stocks. When the corn crop had reached maturity, it was chopped up and used for feed to support the farm animals. Harvest time is when we are ripe, growth stops, and we have something to give to support one another. My hardworking dad and grandfather needed rest. Their early hours started at sunup, and they went to bed at sundown. They knew that to bring in a good harvest, they needed rest for their bodies. In the same way, we need to learn the value of resting.

The Jewish sabbatical or season of rest for land is called the Shmita, and it occurs every seven years. Jewish landowners were required by Jewish law to rest the land. They were to give the ground a break from harvest. You planted for six years, and in the seventh year, you let the ground rest—no planting or harvesting in the seventh year. This made the ground more fertile and allowed minerals to build up in the soil. If they did not rest the field, then the harvest suffered. We need rest to produce our best. Of all the challenges in life, listening to our bodies and not working long hours are among the hardest. As humans, we test our limits, pushing to go the extra mile.

Many times, I have overbooked (we all do). But I am much better today at listening, planning, and taking a rest. The coffee shops are full of folks pushing the limit with that extra jolt of caffeine. However, the idea of rest must be harvested. Similar to most changes we need to make in life, we begin by planting the idea, watching it grow, and then resting in His plan. But we need to plan for rest for it to happen. God wants you to find rest for your soul. Set aside restful times like a weekly Sabbath day, and plan breaks or short times of rest each day. Try fasting from your phone and from being in a hurry. I have a saying, "Hurry makes life blurry." Slow down, and don't race against time. A beautiful life is one that flows each day.

Rest and fasting are similar in that the idea is to take a break or to rest from something. Intermittent fasting as a way of resting our digestive system is gaining popularity and helping many with weight and health issues. The Bible talks about fasting as an act of consecration to the Lord. Resting is a form of fasting from things. Like the ground, it can be good for us and good for the harvest.

The harvest has seasons. There is order in God's plan, and there should be order in your life. One way to bring order is to get your house in order. Clear the stuff, declutter, organize, and minimize are all terms for "Get rid of it!" Things that are not of value take away value. I've had many sample books throughout the years filled with beautiful fabric. As they were discontinued, I collected them. I love to quilt, and quilting takes time, so I had many books. But one day, I was cleaning and stacking these books, and I realized I would never take the time to quilt and use these fabrics, so I gave them all away. The burden in my mind of the task I had set up for my future went away, and my load was lightened. I can't describe the freedom I felt. What is in your home that is a future project, weighing on your mind that one day you'll do? Set yourself free from these *someday* projects. If they are worth doing, then do them right now. When clearing clutter, ask yourself, "Do I love it? Is it useful in my life?"

In America, it is said we have more storage facilities than McDonald's, Subway, and Dunkin' Donuts combined. We are a nation of shoppers, and we love stuff. But a field of weeds cannot bring growth. Just like the farmer needs to clear the field, we need to clear our homes. I know homes that are trying to produce good strong adults; they desire a good marriage, but they never learned how to clear the field or clean out the junk. Make room for the harvest.

My dad passed away from heart issues in 2020, leaving my mom with a mountain of stuff to deal with. He was very gifted in finding trash and turning it into treasure. On the property, they had many storage sheds. Their large home was full of collections, books, and hobbies. Dad loved to cook, and he had over one hundred kitchen knives alone. He thought he would have time to deal with this, but it only added stress to his life in the end. By the time he realized he needed to start decluttering, his health failed. So we found ourselves giving much of it away or selling what we could, not knowing the value. We needed to unburden my mom, who found herself dealing with the stress. One year after Dad's passing, my sweet mom was still clearing and tossing.

THE HARVEST TIME

"They sow the wind, and reap the whirlwind" (Hosea 8:7, NKJV). You reap what you sow. You cannot harvest what you do not plant. If you plant corn, you get corn, so why plant anything less than greatness? I have witnessed words being spoken over a child (seeds planted in their hearts), and later the fruit reaped was a poor self-image. Allow your child to have sprouts of greatness harvested by what you plant. Hosea 14:6 (NIV) says, "His young shoots will grow. His splendor will be like the olive tree, his fragrance like the cedars of Lebanon."

Now that is a harvest. I sow love and kindness to my sweet grandbabies. I want to sow as many seeds as possible and make as many memories as I can. But more importantly, I want to see a harvest of how they will serve and love Jesus, how much kindness they will sow in others, and what talents God will entrust to them.

Bringing order into our lives takes time. You may need help, but you can't have a great harvest with stress and discord. To plow the field, the farmer sets a time. He knows the season, and he marks the day on his calendar. The time is now to plow the field and clear the stuff. The farmer sets aside distractions because he knows if he is not ready, he will miss planting and then miss the harvest. Fast from social media and TV, and get your life in order. Get rid of the stuff that's getting in the way. The mom who wants her teen to keep their room in order may need to help her let go of stuff. I love stuff, and I have lots of it. I am not a minimalist who is saying that less is more. But I am saying that if the stuff you have is unmanageable, and if the stuff is the cause of strife and stress in your life, then it must go.

God has a seedtime and a harvest. His harvest is perfect, but His perfection comes from dust and dirt. He takes nothing and makes it beautiful. We become moldable when we understand, trust, and obey. He has a harvest time just for you to bring forth your fruit in your season, so harvest a teachable heart inside you. And clear your heart to receive a harvest of grace and love.

GOD'S FARMERS

In 1960, a nineteen-year-old single mom found herself divorced and with a two-year-old baby girl whom she left with her mom in another town. She moved to Houston, Texas, and worked part-time while attending school. Her ex-husband was living in Ohio and was engaged to another woman. This single mom moved in with relatives but had to ride the bus between work, home, and school. One day, while at the bus stop, she sat beside a sweet lady who noticed her and asked how she was. They talked, and then this woman began to share about the Lord. The young nineteen-year-old knew the Lord, but her life was such a mess. Her marriage at fifteen to a nineteen-year-old Air Force guy hadn't worked, and now, with her baby girl, life was challenging. She opened up and asked this lady, a total stranger, to please pray for her family, her marriage, and her child. And they said goodbye.

The nineteen-year-old was my mother, and I was that baby girl. A miracle came, and my father came back into our lives one month after this bus stop encounter. Three years later, my parents found themselves living close to Houston with baby twin boys. By this time, my mom was twenty-two-years-old. She and Dad dedicated their lives to Christ, and someone invited them to attend a church service in Houston. After the service, a man asked them over for coffee and cake. Many people were there visiting when a lady stopped by. My mom knew they had met before, as did the lady, but they could not remember. My mom thought it had to be the department store where she worked or the flower shop. But right at the end of their visit, they looked at each other, and both said, "The bus stop!" Joan was then able to share with my mother the rest of the story of how her heart had been so burdened for my mom that day.

She went home to her husband, Tom, and told him of meeting this sweet young girl at the bus stop. Joan asked him to kneel and pray for this girl's marriage. God placed a burden of prayer on Joan's heart, and she responded to it. Together, they prayed and planted a seed of faith. I believe that prayer saved my family. Joan and Tom remained lifelong friends with my family, and we experienced a harvest because of their prayers and obedience. This is what reaping and sowing look like. We are all farmers in the kingdom, and we must be laborers. The laborers are few, and the harvest is ripe.

Go out with the intent to work in the field. Leave your home field with the purpose of reaching out and talking to people about the harvest. Wear your overalls and be ready. Hitch up the mule if needed, get a friend involved, book it on the calendar, just one day a month, and see what happens. You do not need a position in the church to do kingdom work. We are not responsible for the harvest, but we are responsible for the planting. The farmer plants the wheat, then believes the wheat will grow. The fields are ripe for harvest, and you are ready!

LET'S DIG IN THE SOIL

The Bible tells us there is a time and season for everything: a time to rest, a time to plant, and a time to harvest. You may be in a season of both. Maybe God is speaking to you about resting, and at the same time, there might be someone at work or in your family whom you need to sow into, and with time, you'll see a harvest with the love of God in the same way that Joan harvested God's love for my family. Either way, ask yourself, "What season am I in? How is my planting season going? How is my field? How am I resting and trusting? Is my field rested and ready for the harvest to come?"

Harvesting and rest go hand in hand. You can't harvest without resting the land, and in the same way, you won't be ready for what God has for you unless you trust Him and commit to adding rest to your life. Take a moment and assess where you are in the areas of rest and harvest. Does your calendar allow time for rest? Do you have room in your day to take time to notice those around you like Joan? If not, see what you need to prune so you can have time to be still and to know God is with you, and you can trust Him to satisfy you with His love.

CHAPTER TWELVE:
WATER OF LIFE

It was our annual school play, and my fifth-grade class was to perform *The Wizard of Oz*. After being selected to be the Wicked Witch, I was excited to play the role with passion and to represent the witch as close to character as possible, but my teacher would not allow us to use actual water in the bucket for the most important scene. How would Dorothy melt me at the end without water? Then it came to me in a creative burst: we would fill the bucket with tiny pieces of cut foil, which would look like water. Dorothy could throw the bucket full of foil slivers on me. It would give the appearance of water, and I would dramatically melt into a lump on the floor. I was perfect for the part, and this was my moment! I was so excited to be in the play, and my mom found the perfect black formal dress at Goodwill. With its many layers of black lace and toil, the very puffy dress could be melted right into, leaving me in a lump on stage.

The play started with me under the house with my feet stuck out in those red slippers. As they were removed, I curled my toes and pulled my feet back under the fake house. I remembered all my lines. But as Dorothy threw the bucket of tin foil at my face, I was speaking, "Look what you've done, I'm melting, I'm melting, what a world, what a world! Who would have thought a good little girl like you could destroy my wickedness?"[13] I breathed in, and as I was collapsing into my black dress of nothingness, I began gasping and choking, trying to get my air. I had inhaled tiny bits of foil! Wanting to be still for the part or wanting to breathe was a choice I had to make.

I could see my teacher in the wings of the stage, and she took one look at me and knew what had happened. I turned a red-blue color as I held my breath, and then I felt faint. But I would not move. Even if it killed me, I was going to play the part. I can't remember what happened next; I just remember seeing my teacher hovering over me as I was choking and spitting out small fragments of foil to the sound of great applause.

THE IMPORTANCE OF WATER

I wish we had used real water during that school play instead of foil. With so many substitutes in life, there will never be a substitute that compares to the goodness and necessity of water. Humans need about eight glasses of water per day because up to 60 percent of the human body is water. Our bodies depend on fluids to keep them going and to move the toxins along. The average human can go three days without water, but then the body is so dehydrated it will die. Here in Texas, we can have some hot summers, and we are always pushing schoolchildren to drink more water and stay hydrated.

Water is just as important as the seed because there can be no harvest without life-giving water. We can plant lots of seeds, but unless they are watered, they will die because seeds must be watered to germinate. Once the fresh buds burst forth from the soil, they are vulnerable to the elements, and again, water is essential for life to continue. In the same way, we need the water of God's Word daily to survive and flourish in our faith journeys. New believers especially need the water of God's Word to nourish the new growth and life of their faith. In Ephesians 5:26, the Bible is referred to as water that washes and cleanses us. Tend the seed of faith God planted in your spirit. Water it daily with His Word, and watch it grow!

When I was a child, our land had an artesian well that flowed from a mountain on the backside of our farm. The water reached the ground surface at its own pressure. My dad placed a steel spout in the rock, and the water was always fresh and cold and never ran dry. All the folks around would drive up and fill their jugs full of this blessing of nature. Dad freely shared our water with anyone who wanted it. As believers, we have a well that never runs dry—an endless Word that refreshes our spirit anytime, day or night. The Holy Spirit is there for anyone who wants the Living Water.

I water my porch plants every morning, and I water my soul every morning with the Word. My porch plants need little water, but I need some Word every morning. Some days, I need more water than others, like my plants in the Texas heat need more water on one-hundred-degree days. I may need to turn to the Word more than just in the morning.

"On the last and greatest day of the festival, Jesus stood and said in a loud voice, 'Let anyone who is thirsty come to me and drink. Whoever believes in me, as Scripture has said, rivers of living water will flow from within them'" (John 7:37–38, NIV). How long can a soul go without water? How long before we are so dehydrated that we can no longer walk by faith? Sunflowers need watering deeply once a week and at least enough water to keep the soil moist, which is about six inches down. If there is not sufficient rainfall in the preceding seven days, the sunflower plant will suffer. It sounds like if you get a good soaking on Sunday, you may go six more days, but I wouldn't plan on it! "O God, thou, art my God: early will I seek thee: my soul thirsts for thee, my flesh longest for thee in a dry and thirsty land where no water is" (Psalm 63:1, KJV). God's Word is the water. We can receive water every Sunday, but like drinking one glass of water a day isn't enough, hearing God's Word only on Sunday isn't enough either to bring you to life. We need those eight glasses a day, remember?

There have been seasons when I needed more water because I was like a dying plant trying to come back to life. I was thirsty. I would be in the Word at 4 a.m. and returning throughout the day this season. However, I've also experienced seasons of just a daily time in the Word. A little in the morning was all I needed. I love reading the Bible, but I also enjoy devotional books from many authors, and I try to enjoy one per year. Plan your watering time, and do not dry out! If you are diligent in taking in the water of God's Word on a regular basis, just like a beautiful sunflower, you will become the rare flower God wants you to be.

DROUGHT

Drought. It's the opposite of a well-watered garden or well-watered spirit. Years ago, I attended an art class, but rather than being overcome with expectations, I was full of doubt. Doubt dries the soul and can wither dreams. I thought there was no way I could master any of the techniques our instructor intended to demonstrate to us. However, the instructor, through her sweet words, encouraged my talent and watered my aspirations, and all my doubts melted away. This happens when we let God's Word wash and water us. The Bible encourages us and helps the garden of our souls to flourish and bloom. Our sweet Gardener, Jesus, wants to increase your growth with His water of life.

Doubt can especially cause a soul drought amongst immature Christians. Immature Christians want to serve God through their feelings. They sometimes throw fits and ask why life is not fair. Others struggle with doubt because of a trauma or a bad experience that made them question God. They want proof of His love, and they ask God to show them a sign. There is always hope for growth, but growth can be painful, and feelings should not lead the way. When doubt attacks, the key to overcome is to go to the water of God's Word. The water of God's word will replace doubt with faith and lies with truth. When you face doubt, you can go to God's Word to wash and restore you. Jeremiah 29:11 is an example of how the promise in God's Word can help overcome doubt: "'For I know the plans I have for you,' says the LORD. 'They are plans for good and not for disaster, to give you a future and a hope'" (Jeremiah 29:11, NLT). His Word brings life and restores hope. When the drought of doubt is affecting your roots, go to the Bible to get restored.

I listened to an interview with Pastor Dr. Tony Evans after losing his wife and partner in ministry, Lois. She was a giver to the kingdom, always doing good on this earth, and she was taken too soon. When asked how he was coping with this sad loss, he said, "I believe what I teach, that God is in control, and He will carry me through."[14] You could hear the victory in his voice, even in the midst of his pain. But this didn't happen overnight. His victory came through the washing of the Word and the building of faith, peace, and hope.

Thomas in the Bible is often referred to as doubting Thomas. Thomas heard Jesus speak of the resurrection, yet doubt moved in, and he needed proof that Jesus was the Messiah, the risen King. And what did Jesus do? He showed him the truth. Jesus showed Thomas the truth that He was the seed that had to go into the ground and then spring forth to life. When Thomas was able to touch Jesus, the Word (John 1), he believed. When doubt meets the Word of God, it can be changed into belief if we receive it.

DEATH BRINGS LIFE

The roots of the sunflower die in the ground, but in doing so, the moisture levels improve in the soil. Similarly, Jesus died so we could have eternal life. Jesus, our Living Water, was buried for three days and rose again to life so we may have life everlasting. The roots He left are what water our souls. A seed must die in the ground for life to come forth. We must die to our selfish ways so we can fully live in Christ.

> *For I fully expect and hope that I will never be ashamed, but that I will continue to be bold for Christ, as I have been in the past. And I trust that my life will bring honor to Christ, whether I live or die. For to me, living means living for Christ, and dying is even better. But if I live, I can do more fruitful work for Christ.*

Philippians 1:20–22a (NLT)

When we die to ourselves and to our selfishness, God's light can shine through.

When we lose a friend or a loved one, there is also a rich deposit left behind. My grandparents left a rich deposit and legacy after they passed. They played a significant role in my life. We plant and sow seeds in relationships and children by faith, and many times we don't see much fruit until there is a bloom of hope. Seeds must die in the ground and receive water before they bring life. It may look like your dream has died, your marriage is over, or breaking that addiction is hopeless, but add water with words of life. A seed that has fallen into the ground and died will grow, rising toward the sunshine. Jesus said, "Very truly, I tell you, unless a kernel of wheat falls to the ground and dies, it remains only a single seed. But if it dies, it produces many seeds" (John 12:24, NIV). So take courage if you've had a seed die in the ground—God can turn it into life!

WATER FRIENDSHIPS

We also need to water the friendships we have. One way we can do this is by choosing to encourage rather than criticize. Being generous with our praise for our friends will help them grow toward the "Son." Another way we water our friendships is by showing genuine interest in the things that interest them and by expressing admiration for their gifts and talents. If you make a mistake with a friend, be quick to pluck the weed and water them with your sincere apology.

Even though you may water your friendships regularly, sometimes a friend is in your life only for a season. One neighbor was only in my life for a couple of years, but they made rich deposits that stayed and influenced my life for many years to come. When we lose friends, they are still with us, leaving a deposit and a change in our hearts.

The apostle Paul understood the importance of watering plants. "I planted, Apollos watered, but God gave the growth. So, neither he who plants, nor he who waters is anything, but only God who gives the growth" (1 Corinthians 3:6–7,

ESV). We can plant seeds by freely giving love to a friend or family member and showing kindness to a stranger, but only God can grow it. Just like a seed is covered with dirt, God will cover the seeds you plant. You are only responsible for the planting. God sends sunshine, rain, and protection.

I was talking with a friend who is an encouragement—always lifting others up and making them feel like the sun is shining right at them. I hope you have a friend like this. I was telling her just what her friendship meant to me. She looked at me and said kindly, "Thank you for watering my flower today!" When sowing and watering seeds, your tender words become life-giving water to sprout unseen roots, which will eventually bring the reward of harvest.

THE POWER OF WORDS

In eighth-grade American history class, I had one of my all-time favorite teachers. This was the only class I ever received an A+. (I need to let you know it was not because of my studies. The teacher allowed an A+ if you memorized all the state capitals and the preamble to the constitutions.) I loved history and reading about the past. The teacher even liked me, and I cared about what he thought of me. It was spring, and spring fever had set in the classroom. I discovered that the best squirt gun ever could be made with nose spray bottles. Running by, you could give someone a quick mist, and I shared this knowledge with my classmates. Before long, we all had one, and we usually got away with our water spray fights.

One day, a boy came into the classroom while the teacher was out, and he got me. I got him back good, and the water fight was on. One student was a lookout, and we settled down right before the teacher entered the classroom. In our fun, we hadn't noticed the water had gotten all over the teacher's desk. He looked around at his class, eyes lowering above his glasses, and in a tone that meant he was angry, said, "Who did this?" The class, all-knowing it was me, froze in stillness. Calmly, he called out the names of the boys in the class that would normally be on the get-into-trouble list.

"James?"

"No, not me."

"Mike?" He went calling out each boy's name. Then a very puzzled look came over his face as he realized it had to be one of the girls. He began at the corner desk and made his way around, calling out each girl's name.

As he got close to me, everyone was watching and waiting. He said my name and then was going to move on to the next girl when he heard me say, "Yes." I do not know what punishment he had planned for the one who got water all over his desk, but I think at that moment, it changed. He was shocked to find out his favorite student had done the prank. He held out his hand, and I handed over the nasal spray bottle. Then, in the most embarrassing way, he went over to the tin trash can and squirted the contents in the can. The bottle had been full, and the sound of the water hitting the can had the class in giggles—it went on and on.

I thought it would never end; I was not laughing.

In many ways, words can be like the water in my eighth-grade spray bottle. God has given us words to encourage others, but if we are not careful, we can unintentionally make a mess. Or we can start out with good intentions but get ourselves into trouble. I was proud of how well I did in that class (and my parents were proud of me), and I wanted to make my history teacher happy. But my carelessness not only covered his desk with water, but it made me feel embarrassed in front of him. Oftentimes, this can happen with our words.

Words have power, and life and death are on the tongue. Seeing words as water gives us a new vision of the power our words have to bring growth. Words can wash away pain, and they can wash away doubt. Words of hope can wash over the brokenhearted and encourage the sick. Our souls need water that flows to others. Get under the spout where the glory comes out—a well that will never run dry!

We have a water filtering system in our home. We desire to drink the purest water we can get, and it tastes better than the city water. Like water, words need to be filtered through our hearts. The words that flow from hurt and pain, spoken unkindly, only bring more hurt. Wounded and broken people have lost their filters. The damaged heart, filled with pain, cannot filter words. It is like a clogged drain, and words do not flow from a pure place. Hurt people will hurt others. May our words, like water, wash and clean with love those around us. My granddaughter Marley was telling me how her teacher was sharing in a small group that words need to be filtered from your mind. Filter them through a heart of kindness.

My dad took his Liberty Bell crew white water rafting in Pennsylvania. My raft had his top salesman, Ron Todd, his daughter, Kim, and Smithy. The guide would stop before each rapid and go over instructions on how best to paddle through. "This rapid is called the double hydraulic. You will need to paddle hard backward. If you don't, your raft will be tossed on that large slab of rock and filled up with water. This will be the most dangerous rapid of the day." The rafts had loops in the bottom to secure your foot so you could reach your paddle over the side. I was paddling hard and thought my foot was in the loop, but as I leaned out, I fell in.

Ron and Smithy were right there trying to reach me, but down I went under the raft and through the rapids. My bottom hit the rocks, and I could not surface. I held tight to my paddle and my breath. The breath-holding contest that I was always doing with my brothers paid off. Two strong arms reached down and lifted me from the water. Throwing my body face down on the side of the raft, the guide began pumping my back so fast that I could hardly tell him I was alive! Water can be powerful. Imagine your words to be the same as the powerful water force that was pinning me under that raft. Don't doubt the power of what you say. If river water can cut through mountains and rocks, then the watering of the Word can cut through the hardest places in our hearts.

Moses spoke to the rock, and water came. We need the Word to water our souls, and we need words that water one another. There is another word that waters our lives, and it is how we water our minds and hearts—our self-talk. This conversation can defeat us daily. Remember the story of Moses and the children of Israel? Joshua and Caleb are the most memorable. They came back with a report that they were well able to take the land. The others said, "No, there are giants, and no way can we take the land that God had promised his people." What promises has bad self-talk robbed you of? *I'm never going to be married; I'm never going to have a child. My dream of being out of debt and owning my own business—can't happen. I'm too old, too young; I lack the right education.* Don't hide the personal promises God has given you; instead, wash them in God's Word. You water with your words—also water with your self-talk.

LET'S DIG!

Although *helianthus* flowers (commonly known as sunflowers) require a lot of water to germinate, they only require an inch of water per week during their growing season. The orchid just needs a small splash of water every week. But how much water do you need to germinate hope for your needs and to address the issues you're dealing with? You may need bucketloads of the water of God's Word.

Carry scripture cards with you throughout the day that remind you that the watering of the Word will wash away and heal every issue or problem you have. Or you may just need a little splash for the day. Either way, get yourself in the Word fully and get under the spout where the glory comes out so you can be a well that will never run dry. Isaiah 43:19 (NLT) tells us, "For I am about to do something new. See, I have already begun! Do you not see it? I will make a pathway through the wilderness. I will create rivers in the dry wasteland."

When I think of water, peaceful quiet comes to mind. When I want to relax, I find water to be soothing to my soul, like an ocean or a bubble bath. I imagine our Savior loved being by lakes and on seas. One story in the Bible that has always fascinated me was when Jesus bid Peter to step out of the boat and walk on water. I've always wondered, *Why didn't the other guys follow?* I think if I'd been in that boat, I would have said, "Hey, let me try it!" It takes great faith to walk on water, and it also takes great faith for us to stand on the water of God's Word for our issues and problems. It takes bold faith and greater belief. We cannot let our situations mask our revelation of who we are and of what the Word says Christ can do in our lives. So get out that watering can, soak in some love, and have faith to believe that the water of the Word can change and rearrange your life!

Let's not be any garden flowers lost among the leaves. But raise up full of bloom the sunshine to receive.

CHAPTER THIRTEEN:
OUR MASTER GARDENER

In Ohio, our farm was close to an apple orchard where beautiful apple trees filled the grounds called Fugate Farms. The Fugate children rode our bus and many times handed out apples. But the memory I have is of their dad's overalls, straw hat, and the shovel he always had in his hand. Mr. Fugate was a gardener. What is the job of a gardener? He plans, designs his land, and decides which plants will go where. He prepares the soil to receive the plants, and he adds what is lacking to feed the plants. He purchases the plants and then plants them. But the most valuable job of a gardener is tending his garden. Tending means to move, direct, or develop one's course. It takes eyes on the ground, planning with vision, and great care to make a garden of beauty.

You can most likely name famous gardens. Versailles in France may come to mind, or maybe the Dallas Arboretum or the Fort Worth Botanic Gardens. I look forward to visiting these gardens a couple of times a year. I visited the Halifax Public Gardens in Canada on vacation, and I could have stayed for hours. But can you name a famous gardener? I can't, but I know my favorite local gardener and have worked with her on many projects.

Also, I can name the landscape companies that do a good job in our area. The best landscape designer I know was a former employee and master gardener at Disneyland. I could tell her what I wanted, and she knew how to make a garden that looked the way I desired. I wished for a woodland feel in my front landscape. She designed it perfectly, with a few varieties of pine trees and some local Texas plants. I could sit on the patio and feel the hint of the great outdoors right in my *cul-de-sac*.

We partner with our heavenly Gardener—to design us and to move us. He tends to the tender areas in our lives and prunes us so growth can come. He wants to grow us from our hearts outward, and He nourishes us with value. He watered us with His Holy Spirit from a well that cannot run dry. He desires to make you a sunflower, rich in His glory, shining where you are planted and reaching higher than you ever thought you could grow. "Take delight in the Lord, and He will give you the desire of your heart" (Psalm 37:4, NIV).

Our heavenly Gardener wants to give you your heart's desire. He planted the desire in your heart, to begin with, and placed those seeds of greatness in you—expose them to the sunshine. I did not know I had the desire to write a book. But my family tells me I've always talked about writing a book and that I always told them I would write a book one day. The seeds were there, and many times, I wrote poems, and they would flow from my heart. I look back, and the desires of my heart have been fulfilled many times.

I remember being nine and asking God for three girls. A sweet family was singing at church with their three daughters. I looked up and said, "Please, Jesus, give me three girls." I asked God for Terry as he was walking out of a church service—"That is what I want, Lord." All I can say is, be careful of what you pray for. "And the Lord answered me: 'Write the vision; make it plain on tablets, so he may run who reads it'" (Habakkuk 2:2, ESV).

You have a green light from heaven. Get that dream on paper, and make that vision clear. Declare it for all to know. When I started writing *I Made the Rainbow*, I had just come off my mission trip to Belize. I was writing each night, most nights, for three to four hours. After about five evenings of writing, Terry asked me, "What are you doing?" I told him, "I'm writing a book!" Terry said, "Well, good, honey." I could hear him roll his eyes, and the thought hit me, *I need to declare this*. So, I shared my vision with anyone who would listen. I would declare I was writing a book for four years. Friends and family would hear me talk about the book, and I even read a chapter to the contractor working on my kitchen.

Many times, I would share with a friend and get crickets, you know, a nonresponse with an awkward pause. I would think to myself, *I need to declare this dream more for myself than for others*. The more I spoke about it, the more

I believed it, and the more I had the desire to archive it. I would have never found my sweet editor, Sarah, and then my publisher had I not done this. I shared it with a client, and she told me that our mutual friend edited books.

This friend had a dream to start a publishing company. *I Made the Rainbow* was her first book as well, and what success she has had. Clear Wind Publishing is off and running. Even when she shared with me her dream and goal to start a publishing company, I told her I would not be publishing my book with her company. But she declared it would be a success, and she did not give up even after I said no. Sometimes, sharing with your friends might feel like you are casting your pearls before swine (Matthew 7:6), but trust God with your desires and commit your way to Him. "In all your ways acknowledge him, and he will make straight your paths" (Proverbs 3:6, ESV). I have a plan for you; it's a good one, and it's good because it's your desire.

The sunflower grows, produces seeds, and then dies. We are here but a short time on earth. Like the grass that comes and is gone. Why not shine? Bloom big. "Whether you turn to the right or to the left, your ears will hear a voice behind you, saying, 'This is the way; walk in it'" (Isaiah 30:21, NIV). You can't mess this up; the only way is not to listen. "He who has ears let him hear" (Matthew 11:15, NIV). The way we learn to hear God's voice is by reading the Bible and by sitting still long enough to hear His voice.

Back in the mall days with my little girls in tow, my middle daughter, the cream in my cookie, loved to hide, and it was a real issue. She would sneak away, find a clothing rack, and get in the center. Quietly, she would stand. I had many hours of "find and seek" Tootie (Taneia). I finally had to stage an intervention. Letting the store ladies know, I left the shop and her behind. I hid outside the entrance until she realized the games were over and she should stay by my side. It worked, and she was no longer interested in being lost and found.

We don't need to be lost and found, but for my sweet girl, it was her way of getting my attention. She had my love and my care, but she wanted more. I see so many women with all the Father's love and care, but they keep getting lost, saying, "Can You prove to me one more time that You care, that You will find me?" Yes, He will, but how much better it is to trust and believe in His love—be still and know.

Instead, we want signs and wonders. I've walked with women who struggled with doubt. "Could God love me after what I've done?" I've witnessed them holding on to any sign of His love. One saw a clear heart in the sky with an arrow, another a shooting star (she was questioning His plan). But how great to just know. After forty years of marriage, I would hate to have Terry question my love for him—all the years, all the expressions of love. I don't need flowers or gifts to know. Flowers are nice, but I know we have a love that is solid. I love hearing the words "I love you" every day. Sometimes, he will say, "Have I told you today I love you?" In fact, that's our song: "Have I Told You Lately That I Love You" by Scotty Wiseman.

DIGGING IN THE SOIL

Do you have a vision board? A vision board is a list of goals or dreams you desire in the days, weeks, months, and years ahead. It is a clear vision of God's plan and purpose for your life. Making a vision board can be as simple as writing your heart's desire and placing it on a corkboard. It might even become an art piece for your home or office. I have a friend, Lori Kroh, whose passion is to create and teach how to create beautiful vision boards based on Habakkuk 2:2 (NIV), "Then the Lord answered me and said: 'Write the vision and make it plain on tablets, That he may run who reads it. For the vision is yet for the appointed time.'"

"Write" means to place it before your eyes. Lori said that only 3 percent of women write their goals. When the king wrote a message, a runner took off with it. Be active and go for it. Lori's boards are true works of art, but her message changes hearts. She is a true sunflower, watering and bringing joy wherever she goes. Get a board, pray for the vision, and write it down. Just make it plain and detailed. Place it before your eyes. Then go for whatever is in your heart.

TRUST THE GARDENER'S PLAN

Our heavenly Father, the Gardener, cannot fail us. He knows the soil you need, how much sunlight you need, and what zone you will grow best in. Sometimes your soil may be a little rocky, or maybe you feel planted in the desert, but the good news is on the way. I loved my little garden. I had a big hat, colorful gloves, and all the cute garden tools. I had to be a gardener; it was my calling and in my DNA. All my grandparents loved gardening, and my mom loved growing many types of flowers and vegetables. So, plant, I must.

I would go to the local nursery with the idea of Martha Stewart clipping some beautiful flowers; she arranged them ever so carefully in a lovely vase, setting it on an equally lovely table. I selected plants just by what they looked like. But I ignored how much sunlight was needed or not needed, how much water was needed, or if this plant did best in a dry spot. I designed my garden with only my desire in mind, not the needs of the plant. Guess what? I failed—many times. But as I had success and found the right plants for the right areas in my garden, the space took shape. I learned to read the label and attend to the needs of the plant and not what I desired. "He has made everything beautiful in its time. Also, He has put eternity in their hearts, except that no one can find out the work that God does from beginning to end" (Ecclesiastes 3:11, NKJV). Even if it doesn't feel like it is what you want, God is always tending to your needs. You will not fail.

I look at the beautiful gardens in our area, and I think of the hours the workmen take and the care and attention all the plants require. The gardeners tend to all the needs of the wide varieties. God does the same for us. He knows that, in time, you will be beautiful. When people see you, they will never know the hours, the trials, the care, and the tending Father God has done to bring forth your bloom that can never fade.

How much soul food did it take to grow you so tall? Only the Gardener knows. We see the beauty of the bloom, we view the loveliness of the plant, and we smell the sweetness of it in you, but you felt the hoe, the Gardener's working hand—the pruning may not have been so easy to endure. Patience is key. Love is patient and endures all things. We only need loving patience.

I could not wait for my plants to grow. I would plant the seeds and then watch and wait, wait and watch. Most of the time, I bought plants with a head start already in bloom. But the greatest reward was a bearded purple iris. This rich purple iris came from a bulb. I planted and waited; it did not disappoint. Every spring, she would pop up her lovely head and grow bigger and better than before. When we sold our family home to a sweet schoolteacher and her daughters, I received a photo one day of that purple bearded iris. She exclaimed, "What a surprise to find this beauty now growing in my garden. I am enjoying your flowers so much; I know you miss them."

My gardening is limited today, mostly in pots. Our townhome has a patio and a small front flower bed. The photo from my old garden filled my heart with gladness that my garden had provided her great joy, and it was in good hands. She enjoyed tending to it as well as I did.

Love is patient and kind. Love is not jealous
or boastful or proud or rude. It does not

demand its own way. It is not irritable, and it keeps no record of being wronged. It does not rejoice about injustice but rejoices whenever the truth wins out. Love never gives up, never loses faith, is always hopeful, and endures through every circumstance.

1 Corinthians 13:4–7 (NLT)

First Corinthians 13 is your garden declaration, the hope of the beauty to come—the *wow* moment, the bloom that you can hope for. If I could have coffee with you, I would say, "Be patient, love with all your heart, and just keep on growing while drinking from the well that cannot run dry."

ETERNAL DNA

Our Gardener not only tends our souls but died so we could eternally bloom. He deposited His spiritual DNA into our spirit, and we can live victorious in Him. When I think of Jesus in the garden, the old song "In the Garden" comes to mind, written by Charles Austin Miles, an American writer of gospel music. In 1912, the song was made popular by Billy Sunday's evangelistic campaigns of the early twentieth century. In 1950, Roy Rogers and Dale Evans recorded the song.

Mr. Miles stated, "It is as a gospel songwriter I am proud to be known, for in that way I may be of the most use to my Master, whom I serve willingly although not as efficiently as is my desire." He wrote 398 songs; many have stood the test of time. My brothers played, and my sister-in-law sang

"In the Garden" at my father's celebration of life. I wept as the beautiful words and memory of him filled the church house:

I come to the garden alone

While the dew is still on the roses

And the voice I hear falling on my ear

The son of God discloses.

And he walks with me, and he talks with me

And he tells me I am his own

And the joy we share as we tarry there

None other has ever known.

He speaks, and the sound of his voice is so sweet.

The birds hush their singing

And the melody that he gave to me

Within my heart is ringing.

I'd stay in the garden with him

Though the night around me is falling

But he bids me go through the voice of woe

His voice to me is calling.[15]

My granddaughter Marley would spend hours tending to her fairy garden on my back patio. She and her cousin designed it in a large planter just for me. Shopping for the little figurines and assorted mini plants gave them hours of joy. During each visit, Marley would take great care moving the fairy houses around the glass rocks that formed a river and rearranging the small table with mushroom chairs. My favorite was watching as she used the tiny rake and hoe to tend the garden areas with care and then the magic as she turned on the twinkle lights.

This is what I imagine our heavenly Father's tending looks like. Tender adjustments here and there while taking His time to tenderly communicate the finished master plan, then adding the light, His glory, that shines through. It is said the artist does not complete the art because the viewer completes art once they see it. The viewer's eyes are the final touch. In seeing the detail and enjoying the talent and beauty of us, we see the master's touch.

"MY GARDEN OF PRAYER: BELOVED PRAYER POETRY" BY HELEN S. RICE

My garden beautifies my yard

and adds fragrance to the air…

But it is also my cathedral

and my quiet place of prayer…

So little do we realize

that "The Glory and The Power"

of He who made the universe

lies hidden in a flower.[16]

I prayed for God to give me His vision for how I could help young women see themselves as God the Father sees them. Young women should treat themselves as daughters of the King and not put themselves down. I want God's beloved daughters to honor who they truly are. I want them to understand how to stand out in the field in which they are planted while declaring their gifts and talents. The way we view ourselves directly affects how we view others. We tell one another to show kindness and love, but we have none for ourselves. The sunflower vision is a gift and a way to give us a picture of who we are as King's daughters.

Moses had an encounter with God, and he was allowed to see God as He walked away. His light and His brightness would have taken Moses's life had he fully looked at Him. He still came down the mountain with a glow so bright they placed a veil over Moses's face. He reflected the Father. I wonder how long he glowed. Have you tried to reflect God to a friend or coworker, and you felt they placed a veil over you? The more we know Him, the more time we live in the sunshine and the brighter our glow! The brighter the glow, the more uncomfortable people around you may become. You will stand out more and more. We must live like the sunflower and stand for our Master Gardener.

Consider the birds of the field and how God takes care of them. We can let go of our plan and allow the Holy Spirit to shine on us. There is beauty that comes from a walk of faith and trusting in His seasons for your journey. Have faith for the harvest to come, even when you can't see it. With the sunflower as your guide, you can receive a new passion and understanding for your life. The growth is real, but it can be effortless when we follow the "Son" just like the sunflower.

CHAPTER FOURTEEN:
FRAGRANCE

Have you ever enjoyed a garden fragrance? The smell that flowers exude is a feast for the senses. I love the smell of honeysuckles. They grew wildly over the fence of our family home. When I walked outside in early spring, the sweet fragrance would hit me and instantly change my mood. Scents have that effect on us. My grandmother's home was filled with the scent of lilac—her perfume bath sprays and dusting powder, all lilac. To this day, that scent reminds me of her. Mint reminds me of the farm I was raised on; it grew wild everywhere.

Do you have a favorite scent? Some of the top scents include gardenias, roses, and lilies. Jasmine and orange blossoms make for wonderful home scents. The fragrance from the heliotrope flower is known to hypnotize butterflies, and its blossoms follow the sun much like a sunflower. One of my favorite scents is magnolia.

I love to design spaces that engage all five senses. In *I Made the Rainbow*, I ask, "What does your home smell like?" There is nothing like the warm feeling of smelling good food cooking as you walk in. Or the scent of a candle burning. Who doesn't love the smell of a fireplace at Christmas or the smell of peppermint, pine, and cinnamon? The scents of Christmas add to the joy of the holidays. Scent elevates the world around us and gives an extra connection to memories, places, and events. This is much like the mission event where I had spices from India in a slow cooker that added an extra touch and changed the atmosphere.

Even food aromas bring emotion to our hearts. One day, I was making chili when my youngest daughter, Tessa, walked in. Instantly, she looked at me with emotion in her eyes and said, "That smell reminds me of our old home." Because of the power of scents, even realtors will tell you to bake chocolate chip cookies to make your house more appealing to potential buyers. Adding a heart connection to our environment through our senses is very real. Scents affect our mood and health, and entire industries of scented oils are based on this.

Jesus fully engaged the senses in His ministry. He would ask questions; He applied mud to heal a blind man and drew in the sand to bring conviction. Jesus has been referred to as the Lily of the Valley, the Rose of Sharon. Ranunculus are wildflowers in Palestine and almost certainly were referred to by Jesus as the lilies of the field in the sermon on the mount (Matthew 6:28–30; Luke 12:27). "For we are to God the [sweet] pleasing aroma of Christ among those who are being saved and those who are perishing" (2 Corinthians

2:15, NIV). God can smell you. Think about it, Christ sets us apart, places a flame of His Spirit in us, and we put off a scent. So, we need to smell good!

BATHS

I was blessed to stay at Magnolia Pearl in Fredericksburg, Texas. The bluebonnets were in full bloom everywhere. Magnolia Pearl is a clothing line made of unique fabrics and designs. Robin Brown has a design artistry and philosophy that translates into a lifestyle. I stayed in the silo designed as a guest house. There were no showers because she believes in slow living, and baths are the only way to go. I love this idea. Many women ask me how they can add self-care to their day and change their lifestyles.

These women shared with me their love of candles, bubble baths, and walks in nature. Often, I ask women, "When was your last bubble bath, and did you light a candle this week? Did you sit at your table lately and enjoy a meal with family or friends?" As sunflowers, we must slow down, making space for elegant living. We have traded living for entertainment, but we must make a shift. Forget *someday* and embrace today. Enjoy the beauty in what today holds. This is the day to light the candle, take a long bath, and stop and smell the flowers.

Ephesians 5:26 (ESV) reads, "That He might sanctify her, having cleansed her by the washing of water with the word." I think God likes spiritual bath times. I like bath time, too, especially with our grandbabies. The sweet smells of clean baby soaps and oils bring joy to my heart and nose. But as they grow, the sweaty, musty odors after playing outside aren't so pleasant. Our Father knows how to bathe our wounds and heal our stinky places. Allow Him to add the scent of the Holy Spirit over your life. "He saved us, not because of works done by us in righteousness, but according to His own mercy, by the washing of regeneration and renewal of the Holy Spirit" (Titus 3:5, ESV).

LASTING BOXES

I was working with a client who had a kind spirit about her. She would share about her grandchildren; she was so proud of them all. We were working on completing the designs on her new home, which would be the place where she and her husband would retire and enjoy their golden years and their family. Sadly, she discovered her cancer had returned, and there would be no treatment. I cried and prayed with her; this was heartbreaking.

I had to get her home completed, and that was my focus for her. It was good for her to have design projects that took her mind off her illness. She shared with me about her lasting boxes. She had purchased special boxes for each grandchild, and inside, she placed cards for all occasions and little gifts to be opened through the years. The most precious gift was a bottle of her perfume. This costly perfume was the only scent she had worn her whole life. How wonderful to open this box and have the scent of her fill their hearts while flooding their minds with sweet memories of her.

THE ALABASTER JAR

It is believed that Mary Magdalene was the woman who anointed Jesus's feet with spikenard before His crucifixion. Spikenard comes from a flowering plant in the honeysuckle family. I imagine it smelled much like sweet honeysuckle. The spikenard perfumed oil could have been worth 300 pence, an annual wage, in the Roman province of Bible times.

As flowers in His garden, we give off a sweet aroma. Jesus's garden produces a smell that pleases His Father. I get excited just thinking about it. What do you and I smell like? I've grown a few flowers; some made my heart proud. I would show them off to my mother and grandmother. I remember my grandmother sending me photos from her garden of her many flowering plants. How pleased she was to show them off to me.

You are that plant, and the Gardener is saying, "Look, Father, how lovely she smells, how large her blooms." The Father tells the Son, "I'm so pleased with what You have grown. This lovely flower will affect the kingdom and the lost just by her essence." This is why we must stay centered because we are the catalyst, and by our light, others come to know who the Gardener truly is. "Do we smell good? What perfume do we wear?" "You yourselves are our letter, written on our hearts, known and read by everyone" (2 Corinthians 3:2, NIV).

THE PRECIOUS PRICE

Perfumes come in many names and even more prices. The DKNY Golden Delicious Million Dollar fragrance bottle costs one million dollars and sells for one thousand dollars per ounce.

Let's visit the story in Luke:

> *When one of the Pharisees invited Jesus to have dinner with him, He went to the Pharisee's house and reclined at the table. [It was custom to lay down on long sofas at the table.] A woman in that town who had lived a sinful life learned that Jesus was eating at the Pharisee's house, so she came there with an alabaster jar of perfume. As she stood at his feet weeping, she wet his feet with her tears. [Please see this picture; take a moment here and feel her heart. Jesus is lying next to this table filled with food, and she is so moved that she is raining tears, unable to even tell Him what she wants to do, and at His feet, she could not look at His face. Was it shame, her unworthiness of the savior, or was she already broken-hearted knowing this was his last days.] Then she wiped his feet with her hair, kissed them, and poured perfume on them.*

Luke 7:36–38 (NKJV)

An epistle is a letter, and this letter was written on the heart—the mouth speaks, and the actions follow. More than ever, words matter. Sadly, words are often spoken carelessly. It is never wise to use hurtful words, even if you feel strongly or angry. It's normal to feel this way, but words can really stink up a place. Ask God for wisdom on how to speak kindly and in a way that will deposit wisdom, leaving no damage to the heart. "Follow God's example, therefore, as dearly loved children and walk in the way of love, just as Christ loved us and gave himself up for us as a fragrant offering and sacrifice to God" (Ephesians 5:1–2, NIV).

How could the cross be a fragrant aroma? It was the only way we could be saved. A price had to be paid for our sins. We became the children of God, and what was stinky and dead became the sweet smell of forgiveness and the smell of grace! We get to imitate God. To imitate or duplicate means to follow an example or pattern. This idea is rooted in the word "mimic," which is to copy or follow in someone's footsteps. Let's imitate God's love so we can smell more like Him.

> *Then the Lord said to Moses, "Take for yourself spices, state and onycha and galbanum, spices with pure frankincense; there shall be an equal part of each. With it, you shall make perfumer salted, pure, and holy. You shall beat some of it very fine and put part of it before the testimony in the tent of meeting where I will meet with you: it shall be the most to you."*
>
> **Exodus 30:34–36 (NKJV)**

Frankincense and myrrh were more valuable than gold back in ancient times. The Magi in Matthew 2:1–6 brought frankincense, myrrh, and gold to Jesus, and theologians believe He was a toddler at the time of their visit. This showering of gifts did not occur at the manger. I can only imagine that when Mary smelled the beautiful gift of frankincense, she might have thought, *I could have used help with the smells back at the manger*. But God's plan was that Jesus, the Gift and Savior of the world, would enter this world in a smelly place.

Describe what you think you might smell like. Do you smell like a sunflower? A sunflower's fragrance is not floral; they smell more vegetable-like. Candles are my favorite home décor; the smell transforms a space as nothing can.

In contrast to the smell of the sunflower, the titan arum flower (corpse flower) is a floral stink bomb. As a small child, my grandparents lived in a town with a paper mill. At certain times of day, an odor would cover the neighborhood. My grandmother loved to tell me the story of how one day, this odor filled her home, and I placed my small hand on my nose and, looking at my grandmother, I declared, "You stink!" Second Corinthians 2:16 (TPT) tells us, "The unbelievers smell a deadly stench that leads to death, but believers smell the life-giving aroma that leads to abundant life. And who of us can rise to this challenge?" In Psalm 38:5, King David declared that his wounds stunk and festered because of his foolishness. Sin and foolishness can stink up a place, but let us be a sweet aroma to the King. Remember, we are called to be a precious scent to our heavenly Father.

OUR LAST DIG

The quote "Stop and smell the roses" is often attributed to golfer Walter Hagen in the 1956 book *The Walter Hagen Story*, but he didn't mention roses. Do worker bees stop and smell the roses? My Terry will attend a Texas Rangers' ballgame, and before the last inning, he's ready to go because he wants to beat the traffic. Now, I understand traffic is bad after the game, but I love to linger and sit until the end. We paid for the tickets, and I want to see the whole game. Many of us have issues with thinking ahead, so we don't enjoy the present.

Ask yourself, "What brings me joy?" Think of the small things in life that make you smile. When did you feel joy last? What made you smile? Lighting a candle, reading a book on a rainy day, a bubble bath, a long walk? Maybe coffee with a friend or family game night? List three things that bring you joy. Now get that calendar and put them down: one, two, three. Now, they are booked.

When you take that bubble bath, then plan the next date to revisit the tub. This sounds crazy to book time for self-care, but when you have been neglected for so long, it will be hard to think of your needs right now. At some point, it may become easy to find joy every day. No one will plan this for you or value you. Look now at your closet. When was the last time you cleared that field? Set a date for yourself, invite a friend over, and have a fun evening clearing and organizing.

I hope you feel like a sunflower, empowered, through this journey. Show up boldly and bravely in your life, and stay centered in Him. Reflect the sunshine brightly. "Bee" pollinated with love, enjoying relationships. Recognize your petals and organize your life to reflect joy. Stand with strong roots deeply planted in faith, and be watered by the Word daily. Sow many seeds each day, speaking words that uplift all those around you. Allow the Master Gardener to tend you, guiding you in your growth while you smell amazing. Let your aroma fill the air. Plow the field, pull the weeds, and watch the harvest come, but most of all—enjoy the journey!

NOTES

I MADE THE SUNFLOWER

ENDNOTES

1. Lieutenant F. J. Ricketts (pseudonym Kenneth J. Afford), "Colonel Bogey March," composed in 1914

2. James Clear, *Atomic Habits* (New York: Avery, 2018)

3. John H. Sammis, "Trust and Obey" (Public domain).

4. Zig Ziglar, *Zig Ziglar's Secrets of Closing the Sale* (New York: Barkley, 1984), p. 40

5. Andy Fell, "Sunflowers Move by the Clock" (*UC Davis*, August 4, 2016). Based off Plant Biologist Professor Stacy Harmer, "Circadian regulation of sunflower heliotropism, floral orientation, and pollinator visits," *Science*, Vol. 353, No. 6299 (August 5, 2016), https://www.science.org/doi/10.1126/science.aaf9793

6. Pastor Robert Morris, *Take the Day Off* (New York: Faithwords, 2019)

7. Kathie Lee Gifford, *It's Never Too Late* (Tennessee: Thomas Nelson, 2020)

8. Ibid.

9. Nellie Talbot, "I'll Be a Sunbeam" (Public domain).

10. Fannie Flagg, *Fried Green Tomatoes at the Whistle Stop Café* (New York: Random House, 1987)

11. Jerry Seinfeld, *The Bee Movie*, Paramount Pictures, November 2, 2007

12. Pastor Robert Morris, *Take the Day Off* (New York: Faithwords, 2019)

13. Noel Langley, *The Wizard of Oz*, Metro-Goldwyn-Mayer, August 25, 1939

14. Leah MarieAnn Klett, "Tony Evans on wife's legacy, navigating grief, and trusting God 'even when He's confusing,'" *The Christian Post* (March 11, 2020), https://www.christianpost.com/news/tony-evans-on-wifes-legacy-navigating-grief-and-trusting-god-even-when-hes-confusing.html

15. Austin C. Miles, "In the Garden" (Public domain).

16. Helen Steiner Rice, *My Garden Prayer: Beloved Prayer Poetry* (Ohio: Barbour Books, 2017)